The *Stretch & Sew* Sewing Book

The Stretch&Sew Sewing Book

By Ann Person

An Introduction to Sewing
with Knit Fabrics

Second Edition

Published by Stretch & Sew, Inc.
Eugene, Oregon

Contents

About the Author

Stretch & Sew have become magic words for thousands of enthusiastic women who are now sewing their own knit garments, thanks to Ann Person and the home sewing methods she has pioneered. And Stretch & Sew happened almost by chance.

In 1965, Ann was offered a carton of knit fabric remnants as thanks for teaching a sewing class in her home town of Eugene, Oregon. But turning the knits into wardrobes for her three daughters was not as easy as she had first thought. There were no patterns for knit fashions, no guidelines for sewing knit fabrics. So, Ann began to experiment.

In time, she discovered some basic techniques, taking apart ready-to-wear knits and teaching herself to make them on her own sewing machine. Neighbors and friends became interested and suddenly Ann was teaching her sewing methods to women all over town. Then to sewing classes all over Oregon.

There were Stretch & Sew Patterns in those days, too — butcher paper originals designed by Ann from which copies were traced for her students to use. Somehow, Ann found time to write *Stretch & Sew*, which was to become the first book ever published about sewing with knits.

That was the beginning of Stretch & Sew, an exciting and revolutionary home sewing idea that in a few short years has evolved into an international network of franchised Stretch & Sew Fabric Centers where hundreds of Stretch & Sew instructors now teach Ann's techniques to eager home seamstresses. And, today Stretch & Sew Patterns are printed by the thousands and used — and re-used — in home sewing nooks everywhere.

As Ann says, the success of Stretch & Sew was a combination of inspiration and perspiration. But Ann's interest in sewing and fashion goes back many years. As a child making doll clothes in Eugene, Ann longed to become a fashion designer. To encourage her, Ann's parents enrolled her in the University of Oregon art department when she was only 14 years old.

After college and World War II, when she saw duty as a member of the Women's Army Corps, Ann married Marine Captain Herb Person. Together they operated a resort on Oregon's McKenzie River. Then, three daughters were born and designing and sewing little girls dresses became Ann's favorite hobby again.

Back in Eugene to live, Ann taught sewing classes, coordinated fashion shows, taught oil painting, picture framing, resin casting, and furniture antiquing. Suddenly, that important, unexpected box of knit fabrics focused Ann's talents on a new horizon. And Stretch & Sew was born.

Today, the Person family is intimately involved with the daily operation of Stretch & Sew. While Ann concentrates on pattern design and the selection of knit fabrics for Stretch & Sew stores, Herb has taken over the business end of the company. Her daughters and their husbands are also busy with Stretch & Sew, as are Ann's mother and father.

"As I look back on the past," Ann recalls, "it is a dream come true to be able to share the Stretch & Sew idea with everyone."

Introduction to the Second Edition

How would you like to sew a knit top in 15 minutes? Make pants that are guaranteed to fit? Tailor a jacket without a great deal of tailoring? Or buy one sweater pattern and make eight different sizes?

All this — and more — is possible for the home seamstress who uses Stretch & Sew sewing techniques to create fashions from all the wonderful new knit fabrics on the market today.

But until 1967, when Ann Person's first *Stretch & Sew* book was published, knits were virtually unknown to the home seamstress. And sewing with knits was considered difficult if not impossible. Knits, women said, sagged, bagged, and raveled hopelessly for anyone except ready-to-wear manufacturers.

Ann's ideas quickly changed those attitudes. She discovered that when sewing with knits, the best results came by using big stitches, stretching the fabric as she sewed. And this became the basis of her sewing techniques.

Because of Stretch & Sew, women are sewing fashionable and inexpensive knit wardrobes better and more easily than ever before. It is no exaggeration that Stretch & Sew techniques have revolutionized the art of home sewing and that the first edition of *Stretch & Sew* was a best seller.

Today, Stretch & Sew is the name of a home sewing system that includes not only sewing techniques and sewing books, but Stretch & Sew Patterns and an ever increasing number of Stretch & Sew Fabric Centers specializing in knit fabrics and knit know-how.

Knits are here to stay. New knit fabrics and new styles are introduced every year, calling for up-to-date sewing instructions. Now, with the second edition of *Stretch & Sew*, Ann has written a knit sewing primer that incorporates the latest Stretch & Sew Patterns and techniques. Chapters are organized so that the book can be used as a text in the basic sewing classes taught at all Stretch & Sew Fabric Centers. It can also be read and enjoyed outside the classroom, allowing the beginning as well as the experienced home seamstress to create a basic knit wardrobe while she learns Stretch & Sew techniques.

It is a book for every woman who yearns to sew with knits. Happy sewing.

Basic Principles

Basic Principles

People everywhere love to sew. Whether it be a part of a "do-it-yourself" heritage or a need for individuality, there is a universal appeal about sewing. When I see a beautiful piece of fabric, I cannot resist the challenge to transform it into a fashionable garment. It is as thrilling and satisfying to me as planting a seed and watching it grow. "I made it myself," I say with pride. And, indeed, I am proud when I wear my new garment and hear words of praise such as "Tell me how you did it!"

Women who have never sewn are able to create a fashionable knit wardrobe for themselves. They are amazed to find that they can make a sweater or dress in two hours — and that it is easy and fun.

One of the greatest advantages of knit garments is their comfort. After spending years in clothing that pulled, grabbed, and restrained, we find it hard to believe the absolute and utter comfort of wearing a knit garment. I think we will all agree that we are sold on the easy-care properties of knits: their packability, their long-wearing qualities, and their good looks.

Knowing principles of good sewing provides you with a background and reference before you begin learning to sew with knits.

Thread

The ideal thread to use when sewing with knits is made of 100 per cent polyester or is designed with a polyester core and cotton wrapping. These kinds of thread are designed to give added strength to the seams of a garment sewn with synthetics and the stretch fabrics.

Patterns

Stretch and Sew Patterns are unique. They combine the best elements of established pattern-making techniques with several new sewing features.

Every Stretch and Sew Pattern is a master pattern. Each pattern is printed in a number of sizes and left intact. This feature gives you the advantage of being able to custom-design a pattern to your own size by using a combination of pattern sizes. Using the pattern for several people in the same size range is another advantage for the home sewer.

To use a Stretch and Sew Pattern, all you do is trace the size or sizes that fit your very own, very individual figure.

With many Stretch and Sew Patterns, fashion details are interchangeable. Basic dresses may be made with style variations that are included in the pattern or chosen from another pattern. The necklines on many Stretch and Sew Patterns correspond so that, for example, you may put any of the four collars from the Shell Pattern 350 on the Basic Dress 1550. Jackets can become coat length; pullover sweaters can become cardigans, and the tab front top can move from a work-a-day standby to an extended floor-length dress made of brocade or lace knit — wearable from 5 o'clock 'til you-know-when.

There is no need to buy a new pattern for each garment. Be your own designer by combining, as well as mixing and matching, the Stretch and Sew Patterns.

Fabric

Fabric must be prepared before it is cut. The rule for sewing with knit fabric is as follows: Treat your fabric before it is cut exactly as it is going to be treated after it is worn. If you plan to wash your garment in hot water and dry it on a hot setting in your dryer, you must wash the fabric in hot water and put it on the hot setting in your dryer before you cut. Remember to use soap or detergent for this first washing, as soap will remove any excess dye that could be on the fabric. Do not mix new dark colors with light-colored fabrics as synthetics have a tendency to pick up colors.

If you plan to dry clean your garment, take the fabric to the dry cleaner and ask him to shrink the piece before you cut it.

If you are one of the careful few who always wash dresses by hand, then wash the fabric using soap or detergent and dry it the same way you will wash the finished garment.

Follow these general rules for greatest success:
COTTON: Wash and dry in machine — warm setting.
ACRYLICS: Wash in machine — cool water, gentle cycle. Dry in cool dryer long enough to fluff and lay out to dry. Wash finished garment inside out.

POLYESTER: Machine wash — gentle or permanent-press setting, cool-warm water. Fluff dry in dryer — cool setting. Hang on hanger to finish drying.
WOOL AND WOOL BLENDS: Dry clean.

Check the "Facts on Fibers" chart for more information about fabric care.

Note: The rib knit used as trim on the pullover knit top should not be pre-shrunk. The only exception to this would be when a dark color trim (red or navy, for example) is used on a light fabric (white or light pastel). Because residual dye could be left in the stronger colors, it is necessary to pre-wash such trim. Cut to correct size before pre-shrinking.

What Kind of Sewing Machine?

One of the facts that I wish to emphasize is that nearly all Stretch and Sew techniques can be readily and properly accomplished on any sewing machine, including the old reliable treadle machine still found in homes today. I have often had ladies tell me that someone told them they had to have the newest and latest machine in order to sew on knit fabrics. Sewing with knit fabric would not be so popular if this were true. For some garments, the addition of a zigzag stitch on your machine makes sewing much easier and will add stretchability to the garment.

Stretch and Sew has a wonderful sewing machine manufactured to our own specifications — simply because I knew exactly what I wanted in a machine. I found that I could get some items on one machine and different items on another, but I wanted them all together. This is what has been accomplished! A sewing machine that is precision-made, attractive, lightweight, and which, with a flick of the dial, will automatically make many practical and beautiful stitches, as well as perfect buttonholes and blind hems.

SEWING MACHINE CARE

Your sewing machine is a vitally important tool. It should be kept in absolutely tip-top condition. Remember that it should be oiled approximately once a week. Tension needs to be properly balanced so that the machine stitches evenly. Dust and lint must be removed to keep the machine parts moving freely. Needles need to be changed whenever a point is blunted.

Most sewing machines today are designed to zigzag. These machines have a large hole in the throat plate of the machine. Knit fabric is soft. To avoid pounding this fabric down into the hole in the throat plate, hold both upper and lower threads to the side of the presser foot for the first few stitches. Then you are on your way. If the machine is not feeding ahead, stop quickly. The more stitches you pound into that hole, the harder it is going to be to get your fabric free.

Do not change the tension on your machine. On a well-made, well-balanced machine, there is no need to adjust the tension when sewing on knits. If your machine is <u>not</u> operating properly on knit fabrics, take it to your dealer to have it balanced.

Sewing Aids

Many small and relatively inexpensive sewing tools can be a great help and save hours of time for the home seamstress. Study the notion racks carefully, and do not reject the new ideas that are continually available. Put them to work for you.

Some notions that I have used with enjoyment and convenience are: dress form, magnetic seam guide, folding cutting board, pressing ham, sewing gauge (small ruler with an adjustable indicator), fashion ruler (with curves), hem gauge for turning up hems, and a steam iron cover that protects synthetic fabrics.

Perky Pattern Paper

Perky Pattern Paper is a Stretch and Sew product used for tracing from the master pattern. The 1-inch dots are useful for pattern changes such as lengthening or shortening a garment.

Do-Sew

Do-Sew is a Stretch and Sew product used for tracing from the master pattern and for pattern design. Manufactured from a synthetic material, Do-Sew offers the home sewer a product for permanent, most-often-used patterns. Do-Sew is also used as a stay for zipper and tab front applications.

Elastic

Stretch and Sew elastic, manufactured to our exact standards, is best for your garments, best for stitching, and best for stretching. This elastic is very long wearing, too. I have never had to replace it in a garment.

STRETCH & SEW SWIM ELASTIC (1/4", 3/8", 3/4"): This elastic is washable, dry cleanable, and treated to withstand chlorine. It will not stretch out of shape. It is a very high quality product you can use with perfect confidence in all swim wear, ladies' and children's slacks, skirts, and lingerie.

STRETCH & SEW WAISTBAND ELASTIC (1", 1-1/2", 2", 2-1/2"): This elastic is washable and dry cleanable. It will not stretch out of shape and is firm so that it will not twist or crumple in a waistband. It is to be used in ladies' skirts and slacks with a waistband and in men's and boys' pants.

Perky Bond

A quick way to hem a garment is to use Stretch and Sew Perky Bond. Perky Bond is a continuous strip of multifilament nylon which melts with the application of heat.

To use Perky Bond in hems, first press along the fold line of the hem allowance. Place 1-inch strips of Perky Bond between the dress and the hem allowance with the edge of the Perky Bond along the raw edge of the hem. The Perky Bond will stick to the iron if it is not completely covered with fabric. Bond the hem in position, using a hot iron (cotton setting) and a damp pressing cloth. Iron until the pressing cloth is dry, and you will achieve a permanent bond which is safe to wash or dry clean.

Perky Bond Plus

Perky Bond Plus is an interfacing designed to be used with knit fabrics. It is available as a woven or non-woven fabric with beads of Perky Bond on one side. It may be used in washable or dry cleanable garments. Woven Perky Bond Plus, which is most suitable as a stay fabric or for an especially crisp interfacing, will shrink approximately 1 inch to the yard in length but no shrinkage will occur across the width of the fabric. However, pre-shrinking is not recommended. Simply cut long interfacings on the crosswise grain. Collar and cuff interfacings are usually cut on the bias to provide stretch. Non-woven Perky Bond Plus, which is a softer interfacing fabric, will not shrink and has equal stretch in all directions.

Bonding is done by placing Perky Bond Plus adhesive side against the wrong side of the garment pieces. Using a hot iron and protecting the fabric with a damp pressing cloth, iron until pressing cloth is dry.

Hymo-Type Perky Bond Plus is a very soft interfacing fabric designed for use in garments to be dry cleaned. Pre-shrink Hymo by dipping it in tepid water and letting it dry before bonding. The bonding process is the same as described above for Perky Bond Plus.

Needles

Most sewing machines manufactured in the past twenty years have been designed to take standard sized needles. Needle sizes that we use in our knit sewing are 9, 11, 14, 16, and 18. Size 9 is the smallest and is used only for very lightweight fabrics, while size 18 is the largest and is used for heavier fabrics like leather and, sometimes, girdle fabrics. Size 11 is the average size and is used for most sewing.

We recommend sewing knits with a ball point needle. This ball point needle has a straighter shank and a slightly rounded end, enabling it to enter the fabric without breaking the fibers. Also, the sewing machine is less apt to skip stitches with a ball point needle. An additional help, if the machine is skipping stitches, is to stretch the fabric taut to prevent its clinging to the needle. When all else fails, try cleaning the needle with rubbing alcohol. Occasionally synthetic fabric creates a subtle build-up of residue on the needle, causing the fabric to cling. This, in turn, holds the thread so that it will not catch the bobbin thread as it passes underneath. Changing the needle often is an essential part of sewing satisfactorily on knits.

To compare European and American needle sizes, the following chart will be helpful:

American Size	European Size
9	70
11	80
14	90
16	100
18	110

In addition to the number sizes, the ball point needles have an additional sizing that indicates the size of the ball point:

SES — fine
SUK — medium
SKG — heavy

Pattern Weights

A time-saving device that works so well is to use our Stretch and Sew pattern weights when cutting out fabrics.

Pins

Let me stress the importance of buying the best pins. A favorite of mine is a very sharp, long, steel pin with a glass head. It is extremely important to use a sharp pin in sewing with knits; a dull pin can snag and tear your fabric.

Shears

Accuracy in cutting your garment is essential, but this is difficult unless you have good sharp shears.

Today we have a fine carbon steel shear designed especially for Stretch and Sew. The shear has a knife edge and will cut numerous layers of fabric with ease.

Cutting Techniques

To the most frequently asked question, "But, if I cut it, won't it run?", the answer is "No!" Most knits have been processed to prevent running. In addition to this, most of the synthetic yarns are texturized which causes an interlocking of the stitches and eliminates running. Occasionally, a nylon or polyester yarn that has been designed to have a very silky appearance will have a tendency to run if stress is applied to the cut edge. However, if the fabric is handled with care, running will not occur. Knits will only run from the bottom up. Check the fabric you are going to be working with. If it has a tendency to run, place all the pattern pieces in the same direction so that the "running edge" is at the lower edge of the garment.

When you sew with knits, the greater amount of stretch should go around the body of the garment — across the pattern. Check the stretch and place the pattern according to the rule above. Also, check the crease in the fabric. Sometimes this crease is pressed in during the manufacturing process and becomes permanent. If your fabric has a permanent crease (as will be found in single knit cotton, for example), do not use it as the fold indicated on the pattern. Re-fold your fabric to avoid this original crease and place your pattern on the new fold. The permanent crease may be used as the sleeve crease.

Cutting through a double thickness of fabric will automatically give a right and left side. With a knit that has a predominant pattern, cut one thickness at a time. Be certain to turn each pattern piece over to get both a right and left side.

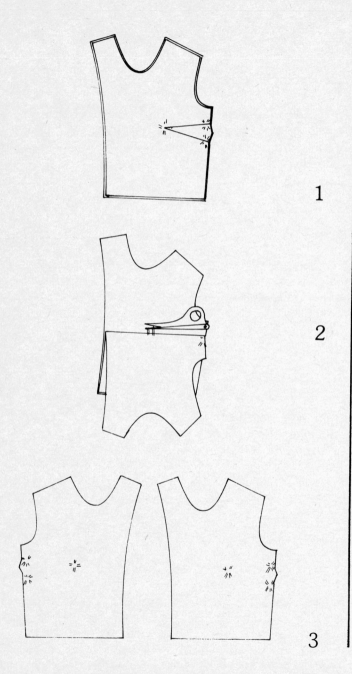

1

2

3

Construction Marking

To insure proper fit and ease in your garment, it is important that you transfer the marks from the pattern to the fabric. This is easily done with a piece of chalk, a sliver of hand soap, or with tailor tacks. I do not recommend using a tracing wheel since the carbon marks do not always come out of the fabric and could ruin an otherwise beautiful garment. A tracing wheel may also cut the threads of a knit fabric and cause holes or runs to begin in the fabric. Chalk or soap marks are not as permanent as tailor tacks, so if the garment will be handled a lot, they would not be satisfactory. For immediate use, they work beautifully. A tailor tack is easily done and more durable during construction. It is easily removed upon completion.

To make tailor tacks, thread a hand sewing needle with a long piece of contrasting thread. Double it over but do not knot the ends. One trick I have found that works well is to use four-strand darning cotton. However, this is often not available in today's home. I prefer the darning cotton because it is not mercerized and will not slip out of the fabric as readily as finer, mercerized thread. Stitch through the pattern and all the layers of fabric, making a stitch about 1/4 inch long. Do not cut the thread but continue from marking point to marking point, making a double stitch at each spot and leaving the thread loose between each set of stitches.

After the area is marked, cut the loose thread between stitches so that there are no stitches joined together. (Fig. 1)

Carefully remove the pattern. Then, separate the garment slightly. Cut the thread between the pieces of fabric, leaving ends of thread on both of them. (Figs. 2 & 3) After you have finished sewing, these threads are easily pulled out without leaving marks.

Pressing Techniques

Pressing is, and always has been, the secret of a beautifully finished garment. The pressing must be a part of the construction and not a last minute thought after the garment is completed. Every seam must be pressed as it is sewn. It is impossible to sew efficiently without an ironing board at your side.

I feel that a great deal of the reluctance to press is due to the fact that many of the fabrics we are working with today are synthetics and we are not always sure just how to treat them. One of the popular synthetics is polyester. Polyesters have been heat set at a high degree of temperature to prevent wrinkling and to insure good shape recovery in the stretch. Each seam must be heat set again. Steam helps the iron achieve the necessary temperature and a pressing cloth protects the synthetic fibers of the fabric.

The type of pressing cloth can be a matter of personal preference as long as you do use one. I like to use a piece of old sheeting because it dampens the fabric so evenly. Friends who are great seamstresses tell me there is nothing like a piece of cheesecloth. A gentleman tailor I know recommends a piece of muslin that has been boiled for two hours. Because it is so important to get sufficient steam when pressing knits, I prefer to be able to saturate the pressing cloth rather than use a chemically treated cloth that prevents this saturation.

For more convenience in pressing, I keep a bowl of water and a sponge at my pressing board to use when the seam area needs additional dampening and the cloth is already positioned and I do not want to move it. Many times it is important to dampen only the area you are pressing and not the surrounding garment.

The most important thing to keep in mind is that the pressing cloth is between the iron and the fabric at all times. The iron must never be placed on the right side of a synthetic fabric unless the pressing cloth is there to protect the fabric.

Ladies are amazed when I tell them that it is possible to permanently press the crease in a pair of men's pants when they are made of a polyester double knit. A tailor's pounding block occasionally helps to flatten a bulky area, but usually the steam of a damp cloth and a good hot iron is all that is necessary.

Pressing a wool knit fabric is really no different from pressing a woven wool. Again — the pressing cloth is a must. The iron is never allowed to touch the right side of a wool double knit. The pressing cloth must always protect the wool fibers. The damp cloth makes it possible to put a sharp crease in a hem or a lapel. It also helps to eliminate unwanted bulk in a seamed area. I have found a tailor's pounding block useful here, also. The iron's temperature-control dial should be set in the wool zone.

The ability to shape a knit fabric with the steam iron is really only limited by the ability you have developed in the techniques of pressing. For example, a hem with a good amount of flare in a wool or a polyester double knit can be eased with a good damp cloth and a fairly warm iron. The fullness of that flare will ease into itself, giving a beautiful flat surface for hemming. This technique is much simpler with knit than with woven fabrics. Wovens must usually be eased into the desired shape with a line of stitching, but with knits this is unnecessary. Allow the steam to do the work!

Both wool and polyester press well enough to use with a pattern that requires a sharply pressed pleat. A pleat in cotton knit and nylon double knit will probably be more satisfactory if you top-stitch the edge of the pleat 1/8 inch from the fold of the crease.

White wools and cottons have been bleached in the finishing of the fabric so that the fabric will yellow if the iron comes into direct contact with the fibers when the temperature is more than just warm. Again, it is wise to use the pressing cloth to eliminate any danger of yellowing.

Care must be taken when pressing acrylics. If they are stretched out in pressing, it is difficult to get them back into shape. The weight of a garment over the side of an ironing board when steam is applied can be a disaster. The moment the steam hits the acrylic fibers, they relax and the weight of the garment causes the steamed area to stretch. Let the garment cool before you move it from the ironing board. I prefer to press my garments the day before I intend to wear them — especially slacks. Incidentally, new body will be given to a soft acrylic by steaming and pressing it until the dampness is gone.

Polyesters are not as inclined to stretch as much as wool and acrylics, but remember — whatever the fabric, press! Start with a damp cloth and press until it is dry.

Stretching As You Sew

The most important step and the secret that makes our techniques unique from any other type of sewing is the principle of stretching the fabric as you sew. By using this stretching technique, you are giving the seam the same elasticity that the fabric itself has. This is a very important part of our concept.

To accommodate the stretching, you should adjust the stitch length, using a longer stitch than if you were sewing without stretching the seam. The amount of stretch desired and the fabric being used will determine the stitch length and, also, the amount of stretching that is necessary.

Sewing Machine Settings

By knowing how many stitches per inch your sewing machine will produce on any given setting, you can avoid much confusion when sewing. Therefore, it would not be a waste of time to make a small chart for ready reference which indicates how many stitches your machine will produce on each setting.

Many machine settings are in stitches per inch, but others merely indicate 0-1-2-3-4 or A-B-C-D. Once you have counted stitches and written this down, you will always know exactly where to set your own machine when your instructions state that you should sew with a specific number of stitches per inch.

Normally, the longest stitch length is six stitches per inch. If your machine settings are 0-1-2-3-4, the stitches per inch would be about as follows:

Setting	Number of Stitches
0	Stitches in one place
1	20
2	14
3	9
4	6

Knit sewing encompasses a full range of stitches from the long, machine-basting stitch to the small stitches used in curved or rounded areas. The chart below is a general indication of the most satisfactory stitch length for different areas of sewing.

Stitches per Inch	Uses
6	Decorative topstitching, basting, and gathering on heavy fabrics.
8-10	The normal stitch for knits.
12	For tricots and Do-Sew stays.
16	Seldom used on knit fabrics.
20	Normal stitch length for machine-worked buttonholes.

STRAIGHT STITCH: This is the plain stitch that we are all familiar with — the stitch that Grandmother had on her treasured old treadle machine. It consists of two threads, one on the spool on the top of the machine and one on the bobbin (shuttle) underneath the needle. This straight stitch is used for approximately 80 per cent of all sewing and is a good, reliable stitch — strong, but still not hard to rip out should the need ever arise. (Fig. 4)

ZIGZAG STITCH: This stitch is a fairly recent innovation and the beginning of the new look in sewing machines. A zigzag stitch has a natural stretch, so it lends itself well to knit sewing. Zigzag stitching is used for ornamentation as well as utility, and, because of this stitch, many machines now enable the home seamstress to make buttonholes without the addition of attachments. Zigzag stitches, as the name implies, zigzag

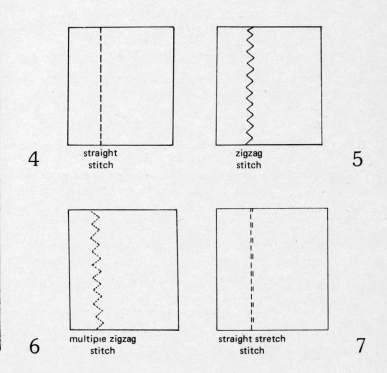

4   straight stitch   zigzag stitch   5

6   multiple zigzag stitch   straight stretch stitch   7

from side to side, creating a wider seam than a straight stitch does. (Fig. 5)

MULTIPLE ZIGZAG STITCH: A series of small stitches in a zigzag pattern, the multiple zigzag produces a very firm seam with much elasticity. This is also a very decorative stitch. The density of stitches makes it popular for mending. (Fig. 6) Multiple zigzag stitching is favored for girdles because of all the pulling and tugging they receive, as well as the constant stretching.

STRAIGHT STRETCH STITCH: Wonderful for strength, this stitch just doesn't ever pull out. In fact, I always caution my students to be very careful before dialing to the straight stretch stitch and to be sure that they want the seam where they are putting it as this stitch is nearly impossible to rip out without cutting the fabric. The straight stretch stitch usually sews two stitches forward and one backward. (Fig. 7)

Seams

When you are working with a fabric that can have a seam pressed open, 5/8-inch seams are allowed. When you are working with a fabric which will not permit you to press the seam open, cotton single knit, for example, 1/4-inch seams are allowed.

It is important when using the Stretch and Sew technique of sewing knit fabrics with a straight stitch that you stretch the seam as it is sewn. When the seam relaxes, it will have the same elasticity as the knit fabric. Normally you will not stretch the seam if a zigzag stitch is used. The exception to this is when you are sewing on Stretch and Sew body rib, nylon rib knit, and swim fabrics.

Buttonholes

On knit fabric the stitches of the buttonholes are not as closely spaced as with woven fabric. In fact, I sometimes tell my classes that a knit buttonhole would be a poor buttonhole on a firmly woven fabric because it resembles a zigzag stitch rather than a satin stitch. The thread of the satin stitch piles up and causes a ruffling of the buttonhole when it is cut.

A little trick I have learned about sewing buttonholes in sweater knit is to work them from the wrong side, or trim side. The trim, whether it is knit or grosgrain ribbon, is always firmer than the sweater itself and much easier to work on.

1

The Pullover Knit Top

Introduction

In 1966, when I taught the first Stretch and Sew lessons, knit fabrics were very difficult to find, and I used to carry fabrics with me so my students would have something to sew on. Sportswear manufacturers were using all kinds of knits to make garments for the public, but none were available to home seamstresses. Today knits have become a way of life, and knit fabrics are much more easily obtained than just a few short years ago.

I learned how to sew with these fabrics quite by accident. Then, when I developed some special techniques for sewing knits, I realized that anyone who loves to sew — and even some who had been discouraged by the difficulty of working with woven fabrics — would enjoy the thrill of creating a garment in a miraculously short amount of time, using these new knits. Since those days, we have taught ladies from eight to eighty in our sewing classes; and we have not eliminated the chance for men and boys to have the fun of learning this new technique of sewing, either. Home economics classes have used our basic knit top to teach boys sewing, and they enjoy these classes as much as girls do.

I believe that the knit top is one of the most exciting garments you will ever sew. Perhaps the ease of sewing on the neckband is part of the thrill, or maybe it is the simplicity of stretching in a sleeve. I know that whenever I use this garment in a sewing demonstration, anyone who has set in a sleeve using woven fabric is delighted to see how simply the garment stretches to fit the sleeve. Even hems are a totally new experience. Because of the openness of stitches in knit fabrics, a machine-stitched hem is easily hidden in the garment. And with the advent of Perky Bond, I have to admit that there is seldom an occasion when I do not bond the hem instead of sewing it in.

The Pullover Knit Top

From Stretch and Sew's very beginning, I have used the knit top as a garment that represents many of the methods characteristic of the Stretch and Sew sewing concept. Today, even with the addition of many different types of fabric, we still use the knit top as an important part of our knit sewing.

Stretch and Sew patterns for knit tops are available to fit all members of the family, from infants to men's size 48. The patterns are basic in their design and, as you progress, you will discover they may be used for many different garments, from a knit sweater to a single knit cotton top.

Knit tops are comfortable, quickly made, and extremely versatile, from casual cotton to elegant polyester or wool for dress-up occasions. Many a knit top of glitter knit has become part of an elegant hostess costume.

The principles taught in the first class of the Stretch and Sew Basic 8 series are the basis of our entire sewing program. In this chapter, I want to share with you the techniques covered in lesson one.

Sewing Tools

Stretch and Sew Fabric Centers display many aids and tools which will help you in pattern tracing, cutting out your fabric, and in the construction of the garment. For your first class, you will need the following items:

Ladies' Set-in Sleeve Knit Top, Pattern 300
Men's Knit Top, Pattern 1750
Children's Set-in Sleeve Top, Pattern 861
Infants' Pattern 850
Perky Pattern Paper or Do-Sew
Fabric: Cotton single knit (Refer to pattern envelopes for appropriate yardage.)
Rib knit trim 2-1/2 to 3 inches for a crew neck style)
Perky Bond, 1 inch wide
Thread
Pen
Tape measure
Glass head pins
Pin cushion
Steam iron
Sewing machine (straight stitch or zigzag)
Pressing cloth
Seam gauge, if desired
Ball point needles, size 11 or 14
A good cutting surface

Determining Your Pattern Size

The first step in making a knit top is to determine the pattern size you should choose. Our knit top patterns are designed to produce a rather loose-fitting garment when made of a single knit cotton jersey with a small amount of stretch. The shoulder line on a knit top is slightly dropped and the crown of the sleeve is more shallow than that on a garment such as the fitted basic dress.

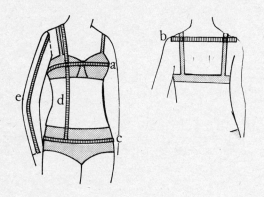

1

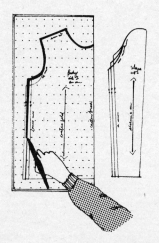

2

The knit top patterns include a large range of sizes. The following measurements will help insure the desired fit:

1. Measure <u>the full bust measurement.</u> (Fig. 1a) This will indicate the basic pattern size. (For example, if you measure 36 inches at the full bust, you will choose a size 36 pattern.)

2. Measure <u>the distance from shoulder bone to shoulder bone.</u> (Fig. 1b) This is a helpful measurement for those who are very narrow or broad through the shoulder in relation to the full bust measurement. It is possible to trace a smaller or larger size, if necessary, to achieve the proper fit in this area.

3. Measure <u>the hips, 9 inches below the waist.</u> (Fig. 1c)

4. Measure <u>the desired length for the top,</u> allowing 1-1/2 inches for the hem and 1/4 inch for the shoulder seam allowance. (Fig. 1d)

5. Measure <u>the desired sleeve length,</u> allowing 1 inch for the hem and 1/4 inch for the armscye seam allowance. (Fig. 1e)

Tracing Your Pattern

After you have determined your correct pattern size, trace this size from the master pattern onto Perky Pattern Paper or Do-Sew. Stretch and Sew patterns are printed on both sides and are to be used as a master pattern. These should not be cut. By tracing, you can use your master pattern many times for different sizes.

For best results, fold the Perky Pattern Paper and place the fold along the fold line on the master pattern with the dots lined up both horizontally and vertically. When you cut the pattern, cut through both thicknesses and you will have a full pattern. This full pattern is much easier to work with. (Fig. 2)

You may trace just the back pattern and then indicate the front neck cutting line on this pattern. If you have traced the neck front edge on your pattern back, a simple technique of cutting down to a point one inch short of the center front is illustrated. (Fig. 3) Cut the garment back with the front neck edge of the pattern left up as illustrated. To cut the garment front, fold down the front neck edge of the pattern as shown.

Cutting Out Your Garment

Place the pattern so that the greater amount of fabric stretch goes across the pattern (around the body). See Fig. 4 for possible pattern layouts.

When a striped or patterned fabric is selected, the garment should be cut out a single thickness at a time. Open up the fabric tube along one creased edge. Position the body pattern next to one cut edge. After cutting, use the cut piece of fabric as the pattern for the second body piece, matching stripes. Follow the same procedure with the sleeve. The stripe at the underarm of the sleeve should match the stripe at the underarm of the body. (Fig. 5)

Construction of Your Garment

SHOULDER SEAMS

Remember to check the seam allowance every time you begin to sew. Seams must be accurate if you are to achieve a true size. Generally, you should double-stitch 1/4 inch seams for extra strength and to smooth out seams which want to roll. Sew the shoulder seams, stretching as you sew. Press these seams to the back of the garment.

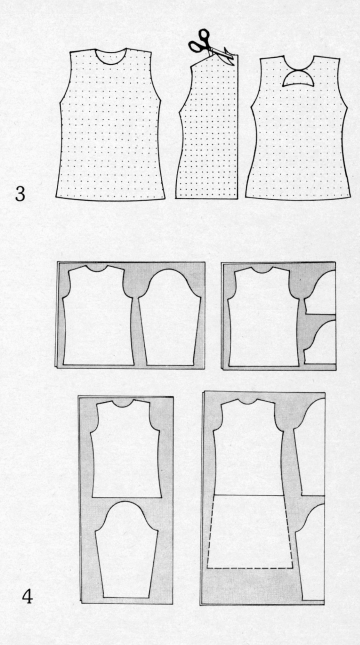

3

4

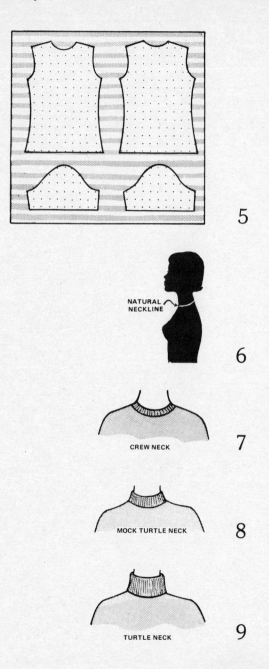

5

NATURAL NECKLINE

6

CREW NECK

7

MOCK TURTLE NECK

8

TURTLE NECK

9

NATURAL NECKLINE

You will hear the term "natural neckline" frequently mentioned in class and described in pattern directions. The natural neckline is the stitching line on the pattern at the neck edge. It is higher in the back than in the front and follows the natural contour of the body. (Fig. 6)

NECKBAND

Choosing the Neckline Style and Trim

The most frequently used technique of finishing a pullover knit top neckline is to use specially made rib knit trim. This trim is dyed to match or coordinate with many fabrics and comes in several fabrics and textures. When using other than cotton rib knit trim in your garment, refer to the section on other trims or neckline finishes in "Variations" at the end of this chapter.

The width of the trim you will need and the amount to be trimmed from the neck edge depend upon the style you select. Fig. 7 illustrates the CREW NECK, in which the garment neckline follows the natural neckline of the wearer. It is a comfortable and attractive style. Fig. 8 illustrates the MOCK TURTLENECK, which extends higher up on the neck. Fig. 9 shows the TURTLENECK, which extends high up the neck and folds down to cover the natural neckline seam.

Two important factors to keep in mind when you select a neck trim will be whether it will stretch to go over your head — if you do not plan to use a placket — and the way it will fit your neck in a relaxed position. A turtleneck made of nylon rib with a 100 per cent stretch will fit a 15-inch neck comfortably when made of a 12-inch cylinder. If your turtleneck is made of a bulky polyester with only a 12 per cent stretch, you may want to use a 16-inch cylinder for the same 15-inch neckline.

When you have chosen the neck style you prefer, the chart below will serve as a guide in your neckline preparation and in the selection of the proper amount of rib knit trim. The ratio described is in relation to the size of the neck opening. For example, if you wish to sew a crew neck style, prepare the garment according to the chart. Measure the neck edge. If the measurement is 21 inches, you will use 14-1/2 inches of rib knit trim. That is 2/3 of the 21 inches plus 1/2 inch for the seam allowance. ⌐ *measure with tape across 1/2 —*

Style	Preparation	Rib Trim Needed
Crew neck	Trim 3/4"–1" from entire neck edge.* (Fig. 10)	2-1/2" to 3" wide, 2:3 ratio plus 1/2"
Mock turtle	Trim 1/2" from entire neck edge.*	3" to 5" wide, 3:4 ratio plus 1/2" for length.
Full turtle	Do not trim!*	8" to 9" wide, 1:1 ratio plus 1/2" for length. (See note)

cut 1 inch off childs T shirt

*After preparing the neck for the desired style, try the neck opening over the head to check for a comfortable fit before proceeding with the neckline finish. If it does not fit comfortably, trim away 1/8 inch from the entire neck edge. Try it on again. Another 1/8 inch may be trimmed.

Note: This ratio will give you a true turtleneck finish. The trim will fold down to cover the neck seam. If a tighter neck trim is preferred, use the ratio given for the mock turtleneck.

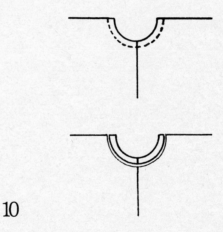

10

Check cotton rib " stretch will need 3 to 4 ratio

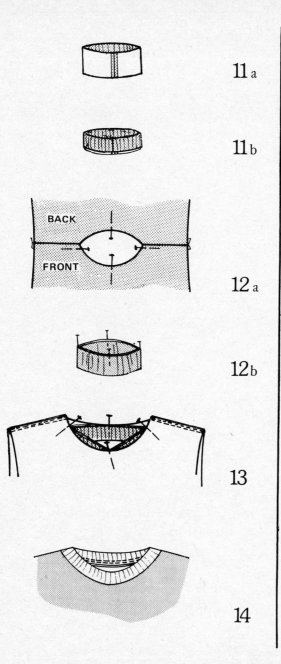

11a

11b

12a

12b

13

14

Applying the Neck Trim

Open the rib knit trim out flat and, putting the right sides together, sew the two ends with a 1/4-inch seam. This will form a cylinder. (Fig. 11a) Finger press the seam open and fold the trim in half lengthwise with wrong sides together. (Fig. 11b)

Divide both the neck edge of the garment and the cylinder of trim into fourths. Mark each quarter point with a pin. (Figs. 12a & 12b) (Note: Shoulder seams are <u>not</u> the halfway point!) If you first mark the center front and the center back, and then match these two pins to locate the quarter points in between, your neckline will be evenly divided.

Pin the seam of the rib trim to the center back, with right sides together. Match all quarter divisions, pinning the trim to the neck edge at each point. (Fig. 13)

Once you begin sewing, do not stitch over pins since this can blunt or even break your machine needle. A blunt needle will cause tiny holes to appear along the seam line. Sew the rib trim to the neck edge, stretching the ribbing evenly to follow the neck opening. Press the seam allowance downward, into the garment.

Finishing the Neck Edge

Three popular ways to finish the neck edge are as follows:

1. Sew a second row of straight stitches 1/8 inch from the cut edge of the neckband on the seam allowance. (Fig. 14)

2. Stretching slightly, topstitch around the entire neck edge 1/8 inch from the seam

line into the garment. This will hold the seam allowance in place through washings. (Fig. 15)

3. Stretching slightly, topstitch, starting at the shoulder sleeve edge. Sew across one shoulder, across the back of the neck and out to the other shoulder sleeve edge. Catch the shoulder and the neck edge seam allowance in the stitching. (Fig. 16)

THE SLEEVES

One of the basic differences between ordinary sewing and sewing on knit fabrics is illustrated in the ease with which one may stretch in a sleeve.

Divide the sleeve in half and mark this point. With the right sides together, pin the sleeve to the garment at the underarm and shoulder. Match the shoulder seam to the halfway point on the sleeve. (Fig. 17) The sleeve will be only slightly larger than the armscye. With the garment body on top and the sleeve underneath, sew the seam, stretching the armscye to fit the sleeve. For extra strength, sew another row of stitching 1/8 inch from the cut edge as shown in Fig. 18.

If you cut your garment from a striped fabric, you were careful matching stripes at the underarm. (Fig. 19) The stripes will match approximately halfway up the sleeve edge. Because of the sleeve contour, the stripes will not match over the shoulder.

SIDE SEAMS

Pin the front and back of the garment together at the bottom, underarm, and sleeve edge with the right sides together. Stretching as you sew, stitch the side seams from the bottom of the garment up through the armscye and out to the end of the sleeve seam. (Fig. 20) Sew another

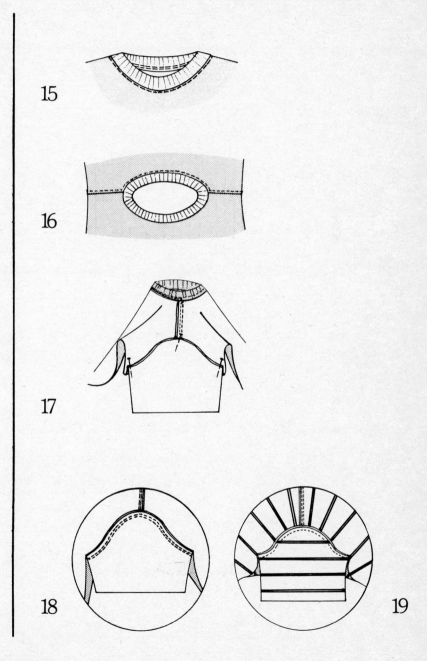

15

16

17

18   19

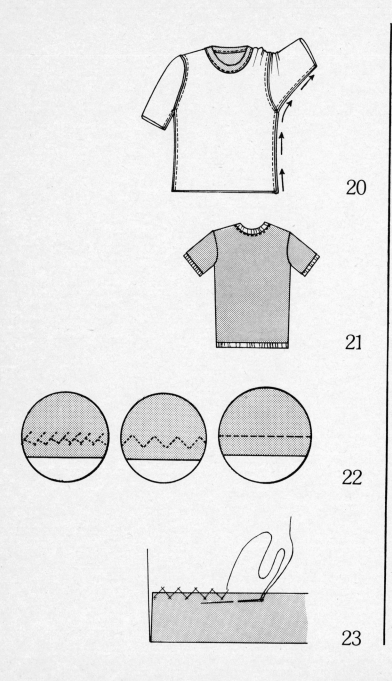

20

21

22

23

row of stitching 1/8 inch from the cut edge for extra strength.

HEMS

Perky Bond Hem: This is a bonding technique which requires no sewing at all. Refer to Basic Principles for instructions on bonding. (Note: Keep Perky Bond inside the hem allowance. It will stick to the iron if not completely covered with fabric.)

Rib Knit Trim as the Hem: Select a piece of rib knit trim which measures about one inch less for every 10 inches of hem. For example, if the hem of the knit top measures 38 inches, the trim should be about 35 inches in length. Rib knit also may be used as the sleeve hem. (Fig. 21)

Machine-stitched Hem: Sew the hem on the machine, using a straight, zigzag, or decorative stitch. (Fig. 22) If you desire, you may conceal your stitching line by careful selection of thread color.

Handcatch Stitch Hem: Using a double or single thread, stitch into the hem and then into the garment, working from left to right on the hem. The individual stitches are taken from right to left, creating a zigzag stitch done by hand. (Fig. 23)

Variations

NECKLINE FINISHES

If you are using a nylon rib trim, you will find that it has more stretch than cotton. You may want to use 1 to 2 inches <u>less</u> nylon rib trim.

Self-trim may be used if your fabric has at least 50 per cent stretch. Using a ratio of 3 inches of trim to 4 inches of garment, you may make a self-trim neckband.

ZIPPER IN A SHOULDER SEAM

This alternative is particularly useful in a garment which must have a smaller neckline than would comfortably fit over the head. It is most often seen in children's wear and, at times, in men's wear. A zipper in the shoulder seam gives a sporty look and is not generally recommended for a more formal appearance. It is best to use a nylon coil zipper rather than one with metal teeth.

Sew the right shoulder seam together as directed in your pattern. (Fig. 24) Divide the neckline into four equal portions. Match these divisions and pin the ribbing to the garment edge, as previously instructed. Stretch the trim to equal the size of the neck opening and sew with a 1/4-inch seam around the neck opening. Press, and topstitch, if desired, on the seam allowance 1/8 inch from the first seam.

24

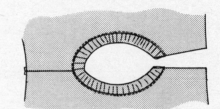

Keep the zipper open when sewing it into the shoulder seam. Place one side of the zipper face down on the right side of the unsewn shoulder seam. Put the zipper tape along the cut edge and the teeth toward the garment. (Fig. 25) (The zipper may extend beyond the shoulder line. After the sleeve has been sewn in, the excess zipper may be cut off.)

25

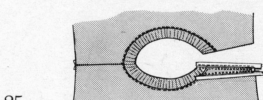

The top of the zipper teeth should be even with the neck edge which is the finished edge of the rib trim, and the zipper tape should extend beyond the edge. Using a zipper foot, sew along the tape, up close to the teeth. Now, close the zipper. Position the second side of the zipper exactly as you did the first side, with the tape along the cut edge and the zipper teeth toward the garment. Stitch the second side.

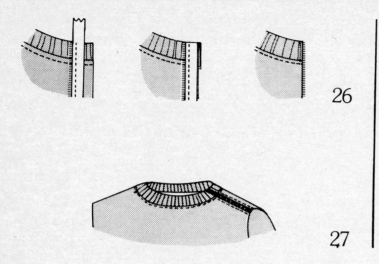

26

27

Set in the sleeve. Then trim the excess zipper away from the armscye.

To finish the top of the zipper, fold the excess zipper tape to the inside of the garment. Fold the zipper into position. The excess zipper tape will be concealed between the zipper and the trim. (Fig. 26) This may be handstitched in place, or the entire zipper may be topstitched, in which case, the zipper tape will be caught in the machine stitching. (Fig. 27)

2

Ladies' Slacks and Shorts
Ladies' Skirts

Introduction

We are especially proud of our Ladies' Slacks and Shorts, Stretch & Sew Pattern 700. This pattern has been on the market since 1967 and has been sewn by thousands of women in the United States and Canada. The style has been modified from time to time to reflect current fashions, but we have now decided to maintain a classically simple pant with a straight leg as our basic fitting garment. And now we have published The Stretch & Sew Women's Pants Book which offers a world of information about making pants, with emphasis on special fitting problems and style variations.

When we were first trying to make slacks of knit fabrics, I couldn't believe that the pattern companies actually had not made a pattern for knit pants to resemble those of the famous sportswear manufacturers. I even entertained the idea that perhaps there was some conspiracy against the home seamstress so she would have to buy her knit pants if she wanted a good fit. There is no conspiracy — we have the pattern!

In addition to the beautiful fit, construction has been simplified so that it is possible to whip up a pair of slacks in almost nothing flat. There is a story I tell my students about the evening Claudia had a date to go on a picnic and found at the last minute that her white shorts were in the wash. The simple solution was to make a new pair — much faster than trying to get the dirty pair washed and dried. I think it took all of fifteen minutes, and the boyfriend was never the wiser as he waited in the living room for Claudia to join him.

One more plus factor: Today, when you visit most Stretch and Sew Fabric Centers, you will be able to try on knit pants to determine your correct size and get instant help in fitting the slacks to your figure. This simple method of having a pair of pants made up in each size has been a tremendous help to all of our customers because it eliminates guesswork.

Ladies' Slacks and Shorts
Ladies' Skirts

For your second class, you will need the following items:

Ladies' Slacks & Shorts, Pattern 700
Queen Size Pants, Pattern 3700
Ladies' Basic Skirt, Pattern 400
Ladies' Skirt With Darts, Pattern 450
Perky Pattern Paper or Do-Sew
Fabric: Knit fabric with at least 25 per cent stretch. Single or double knit will do nicely. (Refer to pattern envelopes for appropriate yardage.)
Stretch and Sew elastic: 3/4 inch for slacks and for 400 skirt, and 1 inch for 450 skirt
Perky Bond, 1 inch wide
Sewing aids listed in Chapter One

Ladies' Slacks

Our Ladies' Slacks and Shorts Pattern 700 and our Queen Size Pants Pattern 3700 are designed especially for knit fabrics and feature our special Stretch and Sew elastic, stretched on the waist, eliminating the need for darts or a zipper. Just five seams and the pants are ready for hemming. What fun to be able to sew a pair of pants in less than an hour!

The initial fitting will take a little thought and the choice of fabric will be important. Once these decisions are made, you are on your way.

Fabric Selection

In selecting a fabric for your pants, the determining factor is the per cent of stretch that has been built into the fabric. The pattern has been designed to be made from a fabric with a 25 per cent stretch. This means if you hold 10 inches of fabric between your hands in a relaxed position on a fold at least 10 inches into the fabric and stretch as far as the fabric will go, you can reach 12-1/2 inches. If the stretch varies more than 10 per cent, the fitting of the pattern will have to be adjusted. Less stretch calls for more ease — more stretch for less ease.

All knits lend themselves to the making of pants — the style you wish to create will dictate the type of fabric. Tailored garments are best when made of a fabric with a firm hand. Pants with a fuller leg and less need for sharp lines can be made from a softer fabric that drapes. Each season new fibers are introduced to the knitting industry and each has its own special characteristics to offer — versatility and change of fashion.

All fabrics must be pre-shrunk, either in the washing machine or by dry-cleaning.

Determining Your Pattern Size

The slacks pattern includes a wide range of sizes. Four measurements are necessary to determine whether your basic size will need to be altered to achieve the best fit. Measure:

1. The waist. (Fig. 1)

2. The hips, 7 inches below the waist. This measurement indicates your basic pattern size. (Fig. 2)

3. Your crotch depth. To find your correct

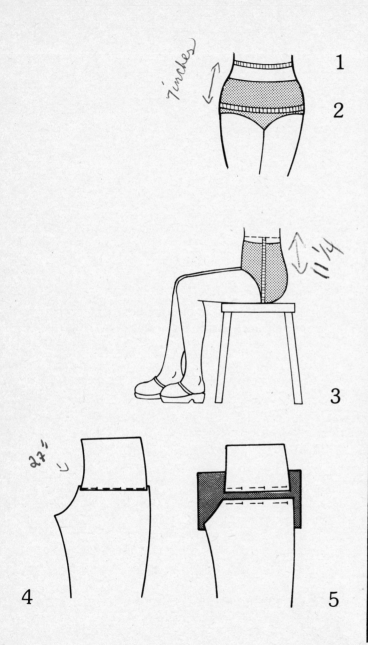

crotch depth, take a "sit measurement" by sitting on a chair or other flat surface, with feet flat on the floor, and measuring from the natural waistline to the surface on which you are sitting. (Fig. 3) Now, compare on the chart below with your own hip measurement and sit measurement with those which are drawn on the pattern.

Hip Measurement	Sit Measurement
30 inches	9 inches
32 inches	9-1/4 inches
34 inches	9-1/2 inches
36 inches	9-3/4 inches
38 inches	10 inches
40 inches	10-1/4 inches
42 inches	10-1/2 inches
44 inches	10-3/4 inches
46 inches	11 inches

If your measurements match those on the preceding chart, proceed with the slacks. If not, adjustments must be made at this time, <u>before</u> the garment is cut out.

On the pattern, a line has been drawn between the natural waistline and the crotch depth. This line is marked "shorten or lengthen here for crotch depth" and is the area where adjustments are to be made. As an example: if your hips measure 34 inches, and your "sit measurement" is 9 inches you will need to shorten the pattern 1/2 inch. (Fig. 4) If your hips measure 34 inches and your "sit measurement" is 10 inches, then you will need to lengthen both your back and front pattern pieces 1/2 inch. (Fig. 5)

If either adjustment is necessary, it must be made on the line drawn for that purpose on the pattern. The same adjustments must be made on both the front and back pattern piece.

The pattern has 5/8 inch of ease allowed, which is the difference between your actual sit measurement and that of the garment. If making pants of a fabric with a very firm knit, greater ease might be required, while some very stretchy fabrics could perhaps be cut with less ease. However, the amount of ease which has been allowed on this pattern has proved to be the most universally needed, and is the one used by Stretch and Sew in their pattern designing.

4. <u>Slack length.</u> Measure from the waist line over the curve of the hip or straight down the front to the ankle or to the length you prefer for your slacks. Add the hem allowance to this measurement.

Our Stretch and Sew Fabric Centers, as mentioned in the Introduction, have available a pair of "try on" slacks in each size. By trying on several sizes, you will find which one is closest to your individual figure. Be sure to wear the undergarments you would normally wear under slacks.

If, in trying on these slacks or in taking your body measurements, you have found a problem which you wish to correct, you should read the following suggestions. These are examples of the most commonly seen fitting problems. Many will be dealt with in your Stretch and Sew class. You may always seek personal help from your teacher, who is prepared to help you and happy to do so.

Work only where the problem exists, such as extra fullness in the hip area, a sway back, or a protruding tummy. Make the necessary adjustments on your pattern and on the garment, and try the slacks on before the final sewing.

Pattern Adjustments for a Perfect Fit

1. Tightness of the slacks across the front or back, resulting in "smile lines" (Fig. 6), can be corrected by using a larger size pattern.

2. Unwanted fullness in the front of the slacks can be eliminated by adjustment at the inside leg seam. Remove 1/2 inch from the front inside leg seam (shortening the front crotch seam). Raise the length of the inside leg seam 1/4 inch (or 1/2 the amount removed) to keep the front and back inside leg seams even. (Fig. 7)

3. Unwanted fullness in the back of the slacks can be eliminated by adjustment at the inside leg seam. Remove 1/2 inch from the back inside leg seam (shortening the back crotch seam). Raise the length of the back inside leg seam 1/4 inch (or 1/2 the amount removed) to keep the front and back inside leg seams even. (Fig. 8)

4. When pants are too tight in the front, creating a V-fold in the crotch area, you may adjust the pattern at the front inside leg seam. Lower the curve in the crotch 1/4 inch and extend it 1/2 inch beyond the present inside leg seam. Taper from this extension down about 12 inches to meet the leg seam. (Fig. 9)

5. When pants are too tight in the back, creating a pulling across the derriere, you may adjust the pattern at the back inside leg seam. Lower the curve in the crotch 1/4 inch and extend it 1/2 inch beyond the present inside leg seam. Taper from this extension down about 12 inches to meet the leg seam. (Fig. 10)

Cutting Out Your Garment

Trace your individual pattern on Perky Pattern Paper or on Do-Sew pattern material.

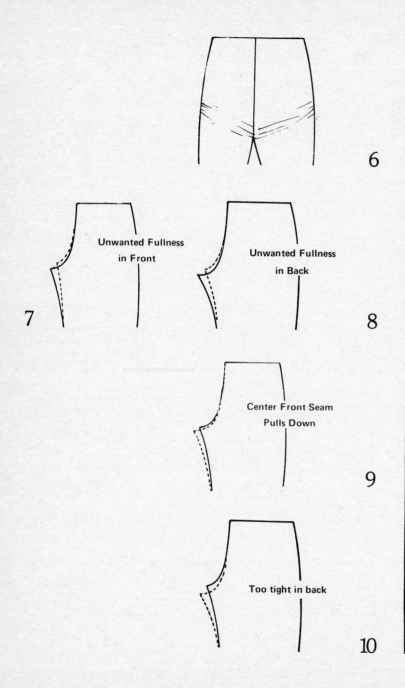

6

7 Unwanted Fullness in Front

8 Unwanted Fullness in Back

9 Center Front Seam Pulls Down

10 Too tight in back

Remember to match any stripes carefully. If you plan to change the basic pattern in any way, for example, to add a cuff, a flared leg, or bell bottom, refer to "Variations" at the end of this section <u>before</u> proceeding to trace and cut out your pattern.

The pattern is drawn so all seams fit perfectly and hems are square. If twisting occurs, it is due to uneven alteration. To check alteration, lay pant back on flat surface. Position the front face down on the back and check seam lengths. Do not stretch to make equal.

Place the pattern so that the major stretch goes across the pattern (around the body). To match a stripe, plaid, or other design in the fabric, it will be necessary to cut each garment piece out one at a time. When cutting one piece at a time, be careful to <u>reverse</u> each pattern piece so that you will have right <u>and</u> left sides. Additional yardage is required for matching patterns and plaids.

Construction of Your Garment

SIDE SEAMS

Remember to check the seam allowance <u>every time</u> you sew. Seams must be accurate to achieve a true size. Place the pant backs, right sides up, side by side, crotch seams facing. Lay the pant fronts, right sides down, on the pant backs. (Fig. 11)

Now, with the right sides together, sew the outside seams of the slacks, stretching the seam as you sew <u>from the bottom of the garment up to the waist edge</u>. Do not stretch one seam more than another because this can cause twisting and unevenness. (Fig. 12)

PRESSING

It is absolutely essential that you press as directed at each stage of garment construction to ensure the best possible fit. Using a damp pressing cloth, press the side seams. Press steadily until the pressing cloth is dry.

To eliminate excess fullness in the hip of the slacks, use the steam of your iron to shrink out the bubble that appears over the hip after you have carefully pressed the seam open. (Fig. 13) Be sure to use a damp pressing cloth and do not stretch the seams as you are pressing.

THE INSIDE LEG SEAMS

Sew both inside leg seams, stitching from the bottom up to the crotch seam. Press the seams open (as above).

You now have two separate units. After turning it right side out, try on one pant leg to check for any additional necessary alterations. If needed, make these changes now.

Now is the time to press creases into your slacks. Match the outside leg seams and the inside leg seams. Use a damp cloth and press until dry. On the front, press from the bottom of the leg up to the waist. The crease should be the center front line, exactly halfway between the two leg seams. The crease up the back extends to the crotch line. (Fig. 14)

Now, insert one pant leg which is right side out into the other leg which is wrong side out. (Fig. 15) Match the two inside leg seams and pin the crotch area in preparation for stitching. Because this is a crucial stress area, you must be careful to stretch as you sew. Stitch, with one continuous seam, beginning at the waist edge at

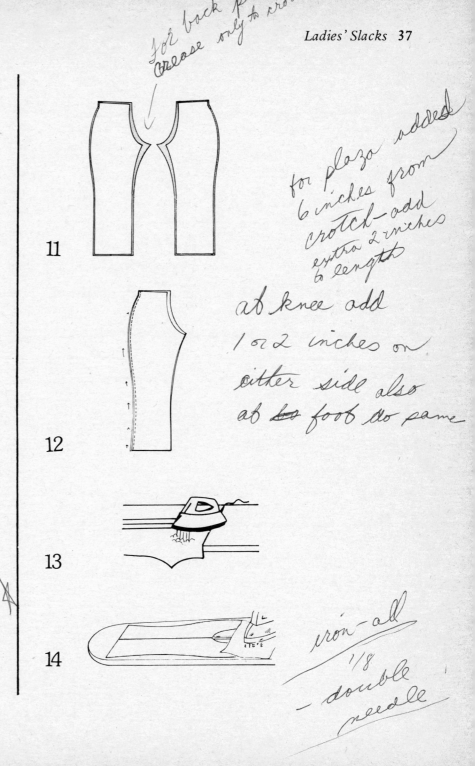

For back pus up crease only to crotch

11

for plaza added 6 inches from crotch – add extra 2 inches to length

12

at knee add 1 or 2 inches on either side also at foot do same

13

14

iron – all 1/8 – double needle

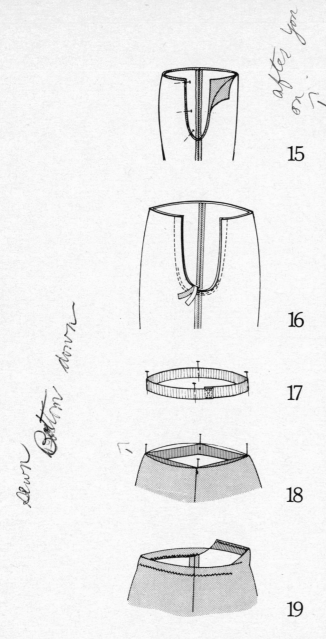

15

16

17

18

19

after you try on

down Bottom down

the center front and sewing to the center back waist edge.

Sew a second row of stitching 1/8 inch from the first through the curved area only—approximately 3 to 4 inches on either side of the inseam. Trim this portion of the seam to 1/4 inch, tapering at the beginning and end. (Fig. 16) With the wrong side out, open the pants.

ELASTIC AT THE WAIST

This pattern is designed to use Stretch and Sew elastic. Following the lead of the garment industry, Stretch and Sew has developed an elastic that can be sewn through yet will not lose its strength.

There is a proper ratio in the waist area for the amount of elastic recommended. Cut a strip of 3/4-inch elastic 1 inch less than your waist measurement. Lap the cut ends 1/2 inch, forming a circle, and fasten firmly with several rows of machine stitching. (Fig. 17) Divide the elastic into four equal sections, marking each point. Match these points to the four seams at the waist edge of the slacks on the inside. Keep the upper edge of the elastic even with the cut edge of the slacks. (Fig. 18)

Using a zigzag stitch (or using a straight stitch and stretching hard as you sew), sew the elastic to the pants, stitching around the entire upper edge. Stretch the elastic to fit the waist. Fold the elastic over to the inside of the slacks. Be careful to keep the elastic and the fold line even. Stitch again, over the first line of stitching, through all the thicknesses, stretching as you sew. (Fig. 19)

THE HEM

Try the slacks on to determine the correct length for your hem.

OPTIONAL CREASE WITH A SINGLE NEEDLE

If the fabric you selected for your pants has a soft finish and you wish to create a sharp crease that cannot be pressed in, it is possible to stitch in the crease. First press the crease in, using a damp cloth and heavy steam. The front crease must be halfway between the inside and outside leg seams. Now, stitch in the crease, beginning at the finished bottom edge of the leg and sewing to the waistband. Do not stretch this crease stitching line. The back crease is pressed in, but usually never stitched in.

Variations

ADDING A FLARED LEG

On the pattern, add the amount of fullness you want, equally on each side of both pant legs, beginning below the knee and tapering out to the bottom. (Fig. 20)

ADDING A BELL BOTTOM

On the pattern, taper the leg in, beginning at the hip. Gradually narrow the leg so that the slacks are one size smaller at the knee. Draw out an equal amount on each side of the leg to the desired width for the bell. (Fig. 21) If you plan to wear the belled leg with higher heeled boots or shoes, cut the entire leg longer. After the seams are sewn, cut the front higher. (Figs. 22 & 23)

PANTS FLARED FROM THE HIP

Draw a flare line on the inside leg seam from the crotch to the hem. Draw a flare line from the widest hip point (approximately 9 inches below the waist). The amount of fullness must be equal on the front and back pattern pieces on both inside and outside leg seams. (Fig. 24)

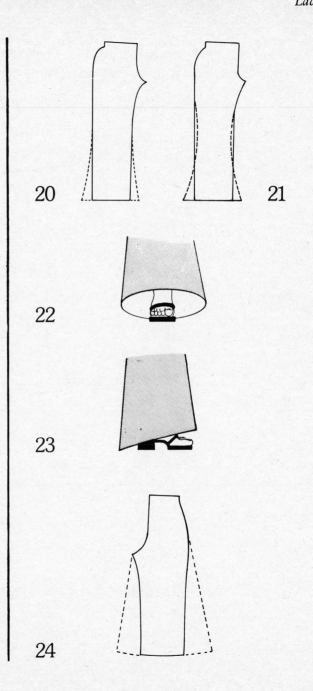

20 21

22

23

24

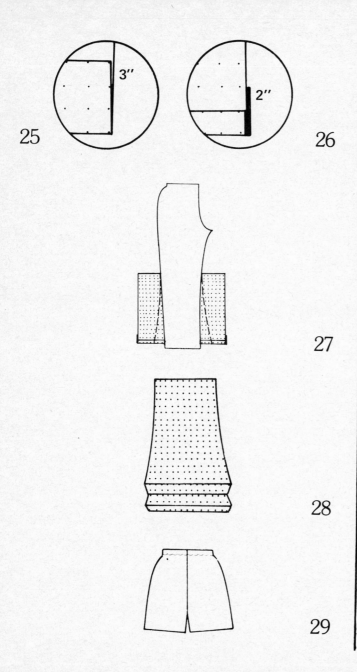

25

26

27

28

29

A FLARED LEG WITH A 2-INCH CUFF

Mark the finished length on your pants pattern. Fold dotted Perky Pattern Paper (22 inches by 22 inches) 3 inches on one edge. (Fig. 25) Fold it again in the opposite direction 2 inches. (Fig. 26) Place the bottom fold on the finished length line of the slacks pattern and attach it with tape.

To create the flare, measure from the leg straight out onto the Perky Paper an equal distance on both sides (from 1 to 1-1/2 inches). Draw a line from the outer edges of this line up on the pants leg just under the knee. (Fig. 27) Cut the Perky Paper on this line, making a new pattern adapter. (Fig. 28) (Remember both the front and the back need a new pattern adapter piece.) Sew the pants in the usual manner. Then fold the fabric like the Perky Paper to create a cuff.

You may wish to attach the cuff to the pants leg by "stitching in the ditch" along the side seam. (To "stitch in the ditch" is to sew from the right side of the fabric into the seam line or as close to the seam line as possible.)

Ladies' Shorts

To make the shorts, trace the pattern as indicated, using the dotted "cutting line for shorts," which appears on the pattern. Shorts are sewn in the same manner as the slacks, using the same measurements and adjustments. (Fig. 29)

Ladies' Skirt without Darts

Stretch and Sew Pattern 400 is a simple-to-sew skirt, designed without darts, zipper, or waistband. Just two seams, elastic at the waist, and a hem! The secret of its perfect fit is in the pressing. You just steam the fullness from the hip area, moving it to the front and back to compensate for the lack of a dart. If you would like a skirt with a more tailored fit and a waistband to tuck a top into, you will want to use Pattern 450, which has a waistband and darts.

Determining Your Pattern Size

Pattern 400 is designed according to hip size. Measure around your hips, 9 inches below the waistline. When measuring, wear only the undergarments you would be wearing under your skirt. Hold the tape firmly, not tightly. Use this measurement to select the correct size. For example, if your hips are 36 inches, trace the size 36 pattern.

Cutting Out Your Garment

Check the length of the printed pattern before cutting out the garment and allow for a 2-inch hem. If your fabric is striped or has a design which you need to match, cut a single thickness at a time to insure proper matching. Cut one back and one front with the greater stretch going around the body (across the pattern).

Construction of Your Garment

SIDE SEAMS

The construction of this skirt is similar to the Ladies' Slacks Pattern 700. With right sides together and using 9 stitches per inch, sew the side seams from the bottom up through the waist, stretching the seam as you sew. (Fig. 30) Do not stretch one seam more than another. Twisting and unevenness of seams could result.

PRESSING

For a perfect fit, good pressing is essential.

30

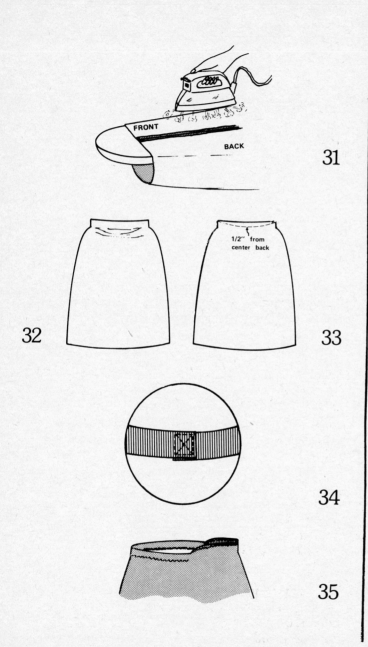

FRONT
BACK

31

1/2" from center back

32

33

34

35

Press the side seams of your skirt open, using a damp cloth and taking care not to stretch the seams as you are pressing. Then, use the steam of your iron to shrink out the bubble that appears over the hip. (Fig. 31)

FITTING THE SKIRT

Try the skirt on to check for fit and to establish a front and a back. Mark the front with thread or a pin. If fullness appears at the center front or back (Fig. 32), remove the skirt and trim approximately 1/2 to 3/4 inch from that area, tapering out to the side seams. (Fig. 33)

WAISTBAND

This pattern is designed to use Stretch and Sew elastic. Measure a piece of 3/4 inch wide elastic which is 1 inch less than your waist.

Cut the elastic and lap the cut ends 1/2 inch, forming a circle. Fasten the ends firmly with machine stitching. (Fig. 34) Divide the skirt top and the elastic into four equal sections, marking each point. Match these divisions, pinning the elastic to the inside of the skirt. You should use a zigzag or multiple zigzag stitch, if available. If not, both the skirt and the elastic must be stretched. The top edge of the skirt should be even with the top edge of the elastic. With the elastic on top and the skirt on the bottom, sew the elastic to the skirt, stitching around the entire upper edge. Stretch both thicknesses as you sew. Turn the elastic over to the inside of the skirt and stitch again over the first line of stitching, through all thicknesses. (Fig. 35)

HEM

Try the skirt on with the shoes you plan to

wear with this garment and check the hem length. If necessary, adjust to the correct length.

Machine hems are often used for sport garments or for a special effect in a hem. However, for a classic, dressy skirt, I prefer a handcatch stitch rather than machine stitching. Again, Perky Bond does an excellent job.

Ladies' Skirt with Darts and Casing

The Skirt Pattern 450 is lovely when made up in knit fabric, and students are always encouraged to try one. There are only three pattern pieces: a front, a back, and a waistband. Because it has an elastic waistband, it stretches comfortably over the hips and does not need a zipper. When selecting your fabric, be certain it will have enough crosswise stretch to allow the skirt to pull on and off easily.

Determining Your Pattern Size

This pattern is designed according to your hip measurement. Holding your tape firmly but not tightly, measure your hips 9 inches down from the waist. You will select the size that corresponds to your hip measurement: for example, if your hips are 36 inches, you will trace off a size 36 skirt pattern.

If, in your own garments, you sometimes have "smile lines" or creasing across the skirt front, you will want to choose a larger size pattern, which will eliminate this problem.

Cutting Out Your Garment

Place the pattern pieces on the fabric so that the greater amount of stretch goes across the pattern (around the body). The waistband pattern must be placed on the fabric so that the stretch of the fabric goes the length of the pattern.

The skirt is made with a vent in the back. Directions for eliminating the vent are found in "Variations" at the end of this section.

Mark the position of the darts with tailor tacks, chalk, or soap. Using a tracing wheel on your knits might cause the carbon to stain the fabric.

Construction of Your Garment

DARTS

As illustrated in Fig. 36, fold the darts, right sides together. Stitch from the waist edge to the bottom of the dart, "chaining off" when you reach the point of the dart. The front darts should be rounded slightly, as shown. Press the darts toward the center front and the center back. Never backstitch in finishing a dart. This could cause a bump of thread or a bubble at the end of the dart.

BACK VENT

Stitching for the vent is done in two rows. With the right sides of the two back pieces together, stitch along the vent seams. Sew from the dots to the waist edge, taking care to backstitch securely at the dots. Stretch as you sew. The inside row of stitching will be 1 inch shorter than the outside row. This inside row is the vent line. The outside line is the seam allowance. (Fig. 37)

When the vent is sewn in this manner, any stress or pulling will occur on the under line of stitching. When hemming the skirt, be certain that the corner of the inside vent is slightly shorter than the hemline so that it will not drop down and show when the skirt is completed. (Fig. 38)

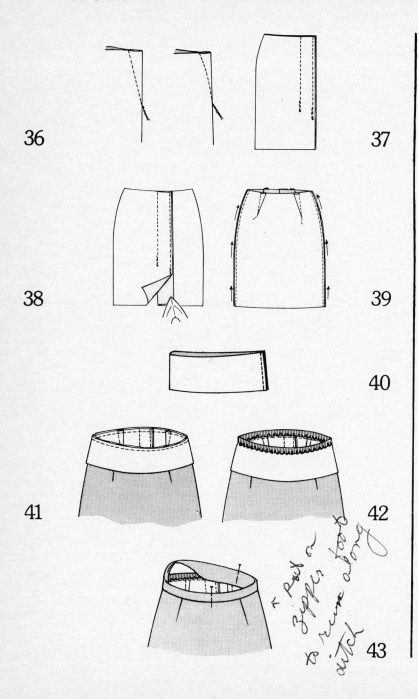

36

37

38

39

40

41

42

← Put a
zipper foot
to run along
ditch

43

SIDE SEAMS

Place the right sides of the front and back garment pieces together. Using 9 stitches per inch and stretching as you sew, stitch the side seams from the bottom of the skirt to the waist edge. Do not stretch one seam more than the other because this can cause unevenness or twisting. (Fig. 39)

WAISTBAND

Stitch the two ends of the waistband together. (Fig. 40) Press the seam open. Try on the waistband to be certain it will stretch comfortably over your hips. Divide the top of the skirt and the waistband into four equal parts and mark them with pins. With right sides together, match the divisions on the skirt to those on the waistband. Firmly stretching the waistband and the skirt, stitch through both thicknesses. (Fig. 41) Press the seam allowance toward the waistband.

This pattern is designed to use Stretch & Sew elastic in 1 inch width. Cut a piece of elastic which is 2-3/4 inches shorter than the skirt waistband. (This will be approximately 1/2 inch more than your own waist measurement.) Lap the cut ends 1/2 inch and stitch securely. Divide the elastic and the skirt top into fourths and mark with pins. Pin the elastic and the skirt top, matching quarter divisions.

With the elastic on top and the seam allowance next to the machine, zigzag the elastic to the seam allowance only. (Fig. 42) This is done to help enclose the elastic in the casing. Fold the waistband over the elastic to the inside of the skirt and pin it for stitching. (Fig. 43)

"Stitch in the ditch" on the outside of the

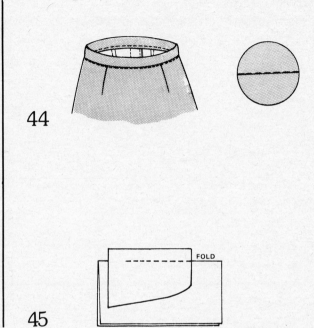

skirt, stretching as you sew. (To "stitch in the ditch" is to sew from the right side of the fabric into the seam line or as close to the seam line as possible.) Be careful to catch the waistband inside. On the inside, trim the extended waistband piece 1/4 inch from the stitching line. (Fig. 44)

HEM

Try on the skirt, wearing the type of shoes you plan to wear with it when it is completed and check the length. Press in the desired hem. Using a machine stitch, Perky Bond, or a handcatch stitch, hem the skirt.

Variations

ELIMINATING THE BACK VENT

To eliminate the vent, place the center back line <u>on the fold</u> of the fabric when you are cutting out the skirt. Stitch the side seams and finish the skirt as described. (Fig. 45)

44

45

3

Ladies' Shell
Zipper without a Seam
Chanel Trim

Introduction

You have made a knit top and it was a breeze. The pants and skirts were great. Now, for a top with a little more style and fit than the simple knit top, we have added the Ladies' Shell with a dart and a zipper without a seam, Pattern 350.

The method for locating the dart and positioning it perfectly for your figure is one that we have used successfully at Stretch and Sew for many years and one that will be a pleasure for you to use.

The zipper without a seam is also a technique I first taught in 1966. It is a simple technique and one that you will enjoy doing. I have even used this zipper technique in classes with young girls because of its simplicity. If you haven't guessed by now — if there is an easy way to do something, that is the way that I want to teach it. I have often marveled at the difficulty some sewing methods use! At Stretch and Sew we will always strive to develop the simplest and easiest technique for sewing each garment; yet never at the expense of creating a garment that appears poorly constructed.

The Chanel trim that we use on the neckline of this garment is also a trick that I learned by examining ready-to-wear garments, and this technique will apply only to knit garments. The raveling of a woven fabric would not allow the raw edge to be exposed; additional finishing would be necessary.

Ladies' Shell
Zipper without a Seam
Chanel Trim

A tailored and classic style, the Ladies' Shell features a bust dart with an optional back waistline dart for a beautifully smooth line over pants and skirts and under jackets. This shell, equally at home tucked in or left as an overblouse, can become the mainstay of your wardrobe. Neckline variations include a simple jewel neckline or one of four collars included with the pattern. The collar styles include mandarin, dog-ear, square-pointed, and Peter Pan. (Fig. 1)

For your third Stretch and Sew class, the following items will be needed:

Ladies' Basic Shell, Pattern 350
Perky Pattern Paper or Do-Sew
Fabric: Lightweight polyester, printed nylon, or other medium-weight knit fabric (Refer to the pattern envelopes for appropriate yardage.)
Perky Bond Plus interfacing (optional — see "Variations")
Perky Bond, 1 inch wide (optional)
Nylon coil zipper, 9 inches long
Sewing aids listed in Chapter One

Determining Your Pattern Size

The Ladies' Shell pattern is sized according to your full bust measurement. By measuring yourself at this point, wearing the type of undergarment you plan to wear under the completed shell, you will find your correct pattern size. If, for example, your full bust measures 36 inches, you will select the size 36 pattern. Trace your

1

JEWEL NECKLINE

MANDARIN COLLAR

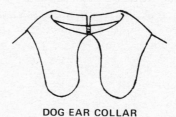

DOG EAR COLLAR

SQUARE POINTED COLLAR

PETER PAN COLLAR

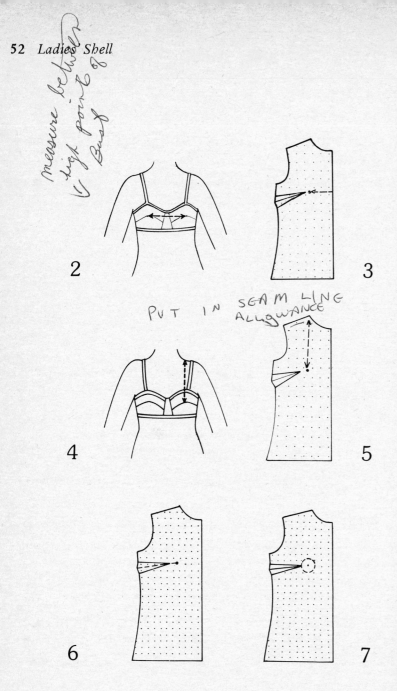

measure between
high point of
Bust

PUT IN SEAM LINE ALLOWANCE

2

3

4

5

6

7

correct size onto Perky Pattern Paper or Do-Sew pattern material.

A well-fitted shell depends upon the location of the dart and your individual figure should dictate its placement. Two body measurements are necessary to determine whether an alteration of the pattern dart is needed.

On your body, measure across your bust from high point to high point. (Fig. 2) Divide the number of inches in half and indicate this point on the pattern piece. (Fig. 3) Now, measure straight down from your shoulder to the high point on your bust. (Fig. 4) Be certain you are measuring straight down and not at an angle.

On your pattern, measure down from the shoulder seamline on a line perpendicular to the previously determined horizontal point. Adjust the height of the horizontal point according to your vertical measurement and mark it on the pattern with a pencil dot. This is the high point of your bust. (Fig. 5)

Now, remembering your high school geometry, use the high point of the bust as your center point and draw a circle around it with a radius of 1, 1-1/2, or 2 inches. (The radius is the distance from a circle's center to its edge.) If you wear an A cup bra size, a radius of 1 inch is usually more flattering. If you wear a B cup size, a radius of 1-1/2 inches is correct. For a figure that requires a C or D cup size, a 2-inch radius is preferable. (Figs. 6 & 7)

When the center line of the dart is extended as shown, it should cross the high point of the bust, and the point of the dart should touch the circle. This indicates that the dart is correctly positioned. (Fig. 8)

ADJUSTING THE DART

If the center line, when extended, is <u>above</u> the high point, the dart must be <u>lowered.</u> (Fig. 9) This is done by cutting along the top and down the side of the dart box, which is indicated on the pattern by a dotted line. Fold the pattern down until the dart is in the correct position. (Fig. 10)

If the extended center line of the dart is <u>below</u> the high point of the bust (Fig. 11), the <u>dart</u> must be <u>raised</u>. This is accomplished by cutting along the bottom and up the side of the box and folding as illustrated in Fig. 12 until the dart is correctly positioned.

The new dart lines which you draw must point directly to the high point but must stop at the edge of the circle, which is 1, 1-1/2, or 2 inches from the high bust point. If necessary, redraw the dart lines to lengthen or shorten the dart so that the end of the dart just touches the circle. (Fig. 13) If the pattern has been cut in order to alter the dart, tape a piece of paper behind the open area of the pattern so that your pattern will be complete and easier to work with.

Compare your other body measurements with those on the pattern envelope. To shorten or lengthen the waist length, use the lines provided on the pattern. To shorten or lengthen the entire shell, alter the length at the hemline.

Cutting Out Your Garment

Lay the pattern on the fabric so that the greatest stretch goes across the pattern (around the body).

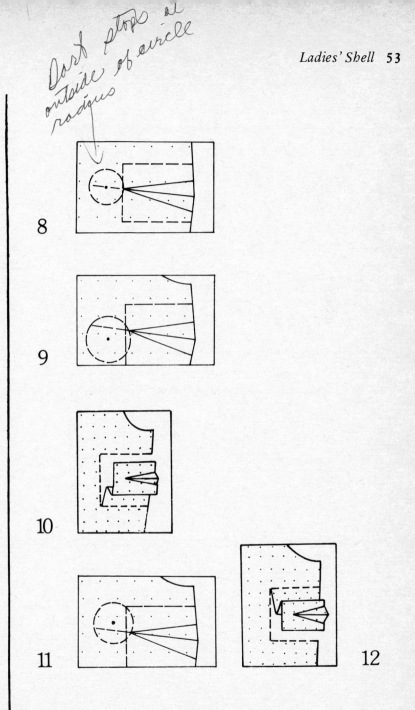

Dart stops at outside of circle radius

8

9

10

11

12

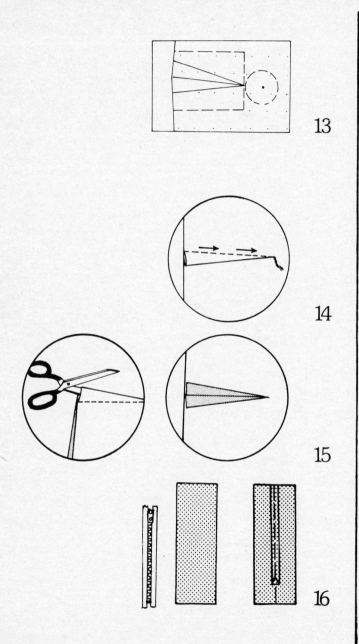

13

14

15

16

Transfer all construction markings from the pattern to the garment pieces. Use tailor's chalk, soap, pins, or tailor tacks. The back dart on the pattern is optional. When I am making a shell that I plan to wear as an overblouse, I do not use the darts. However, for a smooth-fitting shell that I plan to tuck inside pants or a skirt, I prefer using the back darts for a smoother line at the waist with less bulk to tuck in.

Construction of Your Garment

DARTS

With the right sides together, fold the darts along the center line. Pin, and stitch from the outer edge to the point of the dart, chaining off at the end of the dart. Do not backstitch at the end of the dart. This may cause a bump of thread or a bubble in the garment. The last 3/4 to 1 inch of the dart should be sewn close to the folded edge to ensure a smooth appearance in the finished garment. (Fig. 14)

For lightweight fabrics, the bust darts are pressed down and back darts are pressed toward the center of the garment. For medium or heavyweight fabric, the darts are slashed almost to the points as shown in Fig. 15. Press them open. If the position of the darts may be altered, do not slash them at this time.

ZIPPER WITHOUT A SEAM

The exposed zipper with no seam takes the garment out of the "homemade" category and into the realm of fashion garments. The following instructions will enable you to put a zipper into the back of your shell without having a back seam. If you plan to finish the neck edge with Chanel trim, refer to the rules on page 57.

From Do-Sew or a lightweight woven stay fabric, cut a rectangle 2 inches wide by 2 inches longer than the length of your zipper. (Fig. 16)

With a soft-leaded pencil, draw a box measuring
1/4 inch wide by the length of your zipper teeth
plus 3/4 inch. (If you are using Chanel trim, add
only 1/8 inch to the length of your zipper teeth.)
Draw a line down the center of the box and draw
a 1/2 inch wedge at the bottom. Position the stay
on the right side of the garment so that the center
line of the stay and the center back are aligned.
(Fig. 17)

Using 12 stitches per inch, stitch around the
box. Be careful to pivot at the corners to ensure
that they will be square. Clip down the center
line, stopping 3/4 inch from the bottom. Clip into
the corners at the bottom of the box to form a
wedge. (Fig. 18) Turn the stay to the wrong side.
Press, using a steam iron, so that the stay fabric is
not visible from the right side. (Fig. 19)

Put the garment piece, right side up, on a flat
surface. Place the zipper behind the opening with
the metal stop of the zipper at the lower edge of
the box. The box must be even around the zipper.
Pin the lower edge of the zipper with two pins.
The pin points should be directed toward the
metal stop at the bottom of the zipper. (Fig. 20)
The pins will hold the zipper in place without
interfering with the stitching. Using a zipper foot,
sew the zipper, attaching the wedge to the zipper
tape and the stay. (Fig. 21)

To stitch the sides of the zipper, lift the side
of the garment to expose the seam allowances.
Repeat on the second side of the zipper. (Fig. 22)
Trim the stay fabric so that it is even with the
zipper tape.

SHOULDER SEAMS

With right sides together, stitch the front to
the back at the shoulder seams. Between the
notch and the neckline, ease the front to fit the
back, as you sew, with the garment back on the

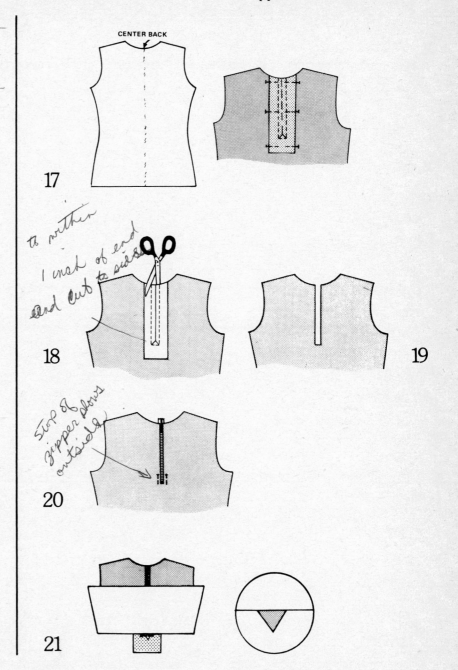

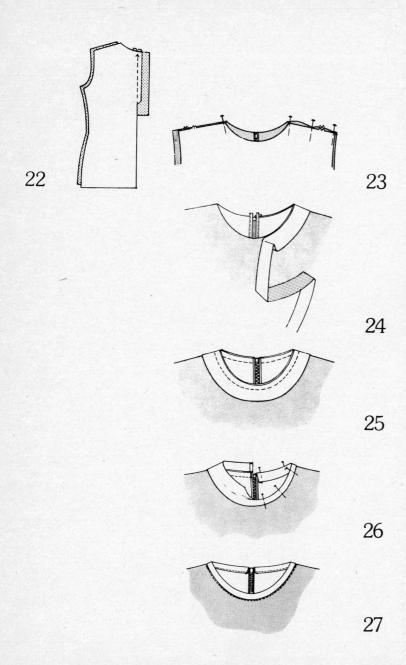

22

23

24

25

26

27

bottom next to the machine. (Fig. 23) Press the seams open.

CHANEL TRIM

The classical and simple Chanel trim is an attractive neckline finish for the Ladies' Shell. Chanel trim is cut with the stretch going the <u>length</u> of the strip of trim.

Cut a strip of <u>fabric approximately 4 times the finished width</u> of the trim. For example, if the finished width is to be 1/4 inch, the strip would be 1 to 1-1/4 inches wide. The length of the strip should be cut the length of the neckline seam. This will be slightly more trim than necessary.

Place the right side of the trim on the right side of the garment, matching the cut edge of the trim to the cut edge of the neckline. (Fig. 24) The first stitching line must be exactly the width desired for the finished trim. Leaving 1/2 inch of the trim extending beyond the edge of the garment, stitch around the entire neck edge of the shell. (Fig. 25) For a smooth appearance and fit, the trim must be stretched slightly as it is applied. Be careful <u>not</u> to stretch the neck edge of the garment.

Cut off the ends of the trim so that they extend 1/2 inch beyond the zipper. Fold this 1/2 inch of trim into the garment. (Fig. 26) Press the trim up and over the seam allowance and down into the wrong side of the garment. (Fig. 26) Pin it into place. The final stitching is done by "stitching in the ditch" on the right side of the neck edge through all layers of fabric. Trim the excess seam allowance. (Fig. 27) Press, using a damp cloth, from the wrong side of the garment.

Remember these simple rules for applying Chanel trim:

1. Trim away the seam allowance. The cut edge will be the finished edge. (For a higher neck finish, you may wish to leave some of the seam allowance.)

2. Cut a strip of fabric with the stretch running lengthwise, approximately four times the finished width of the trim.

3. Make the first line of stitching exactly the width you desire for the finished trim.

4. Stretch the trim slightly on inside curves.

5. Keep the trim relaxed on straight edges.

6. Ease the trim on outside curves.

7. Narrow trim is best for both inside and outside curves.

8. Wide trim is used on a straight edge or with a mitered corner.

ARMSCYE FINISH

For Chanel trim on the armscye, the procedure is similar to that of the Chanel neckline finish. Trim away the armscye seam allowance. Cut a strip of fabric on the lengthwise stretch, approximately four times the finished width desired and the same length as the distance around the armscye. This will be slightly more trim than necessary.

Stitch the first seam exactly the width you want for the finished trim. (Fig. 28) Press the trim up into the armscye opening. (Fig. 29) After completing the <u>first</u> line of stitching and the pressing, stitch the side seams, from the bottom up, through the Chanel trim. Press the side seam open. (Fig. 30) Press the trim over to the inside of

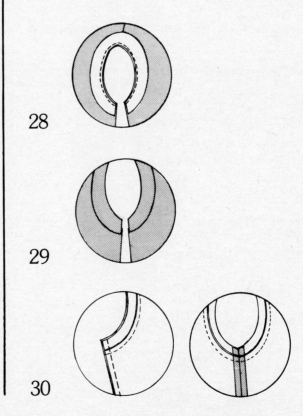

28

29

30

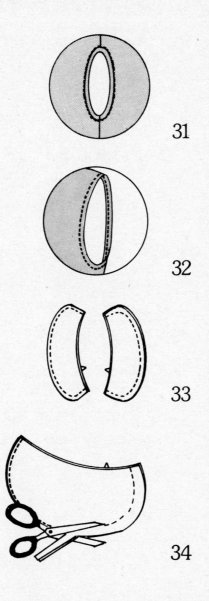

31

32

33

34

the garment. Complete by "stitching in the ditch" on the right side of the shell through all thicknesses. (Fig. 31) Press from the wrong side of the garment, using a damp cloth.

An armscye finish that is especially flattering to this shell is to topstitch. This can be accomplished by trimming 1/4 inch from the raw edge of the armscye. Then, turn the remaining 3/8 inch of seam allowance to the inside and topstitch or hand catchstitch it into position. (Fig. 32)

HEM

Try the shell on to determine the proper length. Press in the desired hem and bond or handstitch in place.

Variations

COLLARS

The Ladies' Shell features four variations of collar styles. You may select the mandarin, dog-eared, square-pointed, or the softly rounded Peter Pan.

When preparing to cut out your shell, transfer the construction markings of the collar you have chosen to your pattern. You will need to cut four collar pieces.

With the right sides together, stitch two collars together along all unnotched edges. (Fig. 33) Repeat for the second two collars. Trim the seam allowance of the collars to different lengths by holding the scissors at an angle as you trim. (Fig. 34) This "grading" prevents a lump in the finished collar. On the square collar, cut the corners of the seam allowance diagonally.

Turn the collar right side out and press, rolling the seam to the underside. This lends a much more finished and professional look to the garment.

With the notches matching and the wrong sides of the collar against the right side of the shell, pin the collar to the neck edge. The collar edges will be at the center front and center back. (Fig. 35)

Stitch the front facing to the back facing at the shoulder seams. Press open. (Fig. 36) With right sides together, position the facing at the neck edge. The collar will be sandwiched between the facing and the shell. (Fig. 37) Stitch the facing and the collar to the neck edge. Grade the seam allowance as previously explained. Turn the facing to the inside and press. If necessary, "anchor" the facing to the bodice with bonding material placed close to the shoulder seam, the center front, and at the center back by the zipper. (Fig. 38) For bonding information, see "Perky Bond Products" in Basic Principles.

ZIPPER WITHOUT A SEAM USING PERKY BOND PLUS

In addition to the Do-Sew stay, I have found an unbelievably simple way to apply the zipper without a seam using Perky Bond Plus.

Cut a rectangle 2 inches wide and 2 inches longer than your zipper. On the non-adhesive side of the Perky Bond Plus, draw a box which measures 1/4 inch by the length of your zipper teeth plus 3/4 inch. (If you are using Chanel trim, add only 1/8 inch to the length of your zipper teeth.) Draw a line down the center of the box and position the stay on the garment with the right side of the garment next to the adhesive side of the stay. The center line of the drawn box should be along the center line of the garment.

Stitch around the outside edges of the drawn box, using 12 stitches per inch. Be sure to pivot at corners so that they are square. Clip down the

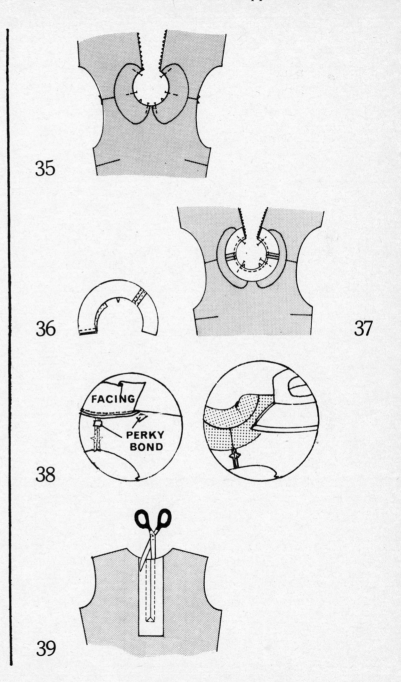

35

36

37

38

FACING

PERKY BOND

39

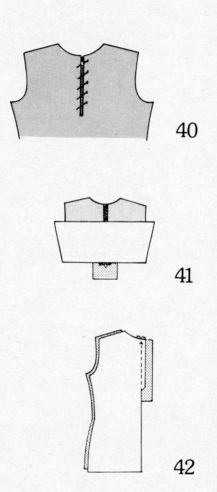

40

41

42

center line, stopping 3/4 inch from the bottom of the box. Clip into the corners, forming a wedge. (Fig. 39)

Turn the stay to the wrong side. Finger press carefully so that no stay fabric is visible from the right side of the garment. Be careful not to touch the Perky Bond Plus with an iron at this time.

The stay fabric is wider than the zipper tape. To avoid sticking the garment to your ironing board cover, place paper on the ironing board. Then, position the garment on the paper, with the right side of the garment up and the opening for the zipper over the paper. Position the zipper behind the open box, with the lower edge of the metal stop exposed at the bottom of the box. Position it with care so that the box is even around the edge of the zipper. Watch the position of the garment and be careful to match stripes and keep them even on each side of the box. The top of the zipper head should be even with the cut edge of the garment if you plan to apply Chanel trim.

To hold the zipper in place, place pins in the garment at a slight angle through the garment, zipper tape, and into the ironing board pad. (Fig. 40)

Lift up the bottom of the garment exposing the wedge. (Fig. 41) Using a dampened pressing cloth, press the wedge, bonding it into place.

Fold back each side, bonding it in the same manner. (Fig. 42)

Trim the stay back to the zipper tape, leaving a very stable, yet attractive, zipper. The bonding will hold the zipper in place, but you may stitch for reinforcement as described earlier in this chapter under "The Zipper Without a Seam."

4

The Raglan Sleeve Knit Top
The Invisible Zipper
Zipper in a Turtleneck

64

Introduction

Now that you have learned many of the great and practical techniques of sewing with knits, you will enjoy using them to create a Raglan Sleeve Top. This is a classic style which lends itself to almost any stretch fabric. The ladies' pattern includes a square neck adapter. To create a neck opening to accommodate a fabric with little stretch, try a hidden zipper in one of the raglan sleeve seams.

The Raglan Sleeve Top is particularly good-looking in a wide-stripe fabric, with the stripes matched exactly, to emphasize the squared style. A bold stripe makes a rugged looking top for men. For yourself, you might like to try a border print. By selecting different textures, colors, and patterns of knit fabrics, you may create many garments from this one basic pattern.

The Raglan Sleeve Top is especially suitable for children, as they are outgrown less quickly than tops with set-in sleeves. This is good news for the economical mother who sews.

The Raglan Sleeve Knit Top
The Invisible Zipper
Zipper in a Turtleneck

For your fourth Stretch and Sew class, you will need the following items:

Ladies' Raglan Sleeve Top, Pattern 200
Men's Raglan Sleeve Top, Pattern 1710
Children's Raglan Sleeve Top, Pattern 862
Infants' Pattern 850
Perky Pattern Paper or Do-Sew
Fabric: Lightweight polyester, double knit or single knit cotton or blends, polyester and blends, acrylics, wool, and sweater bodies. (Refer to the pattern envelopes for appropriate yardage.)
Perky Bond, 1 inch wide (optional)
Invisible zipper and invisible zipper foot (optional for the raglan square neck)
12-inch zipper (optional for the turtleneck)
Rib knit trim (optional for a crew neck, mock turtleneck, or turtleneck)
Sewing aids listed in Chapter One

Determining Your Pattern Size

The Ladies' Raglan Sleeve Top Pattern 200 is sized according to the full bust measurement. If your full bust measurement is 36 inches, for example, you will select a size 36 pattern.

Tracing and Cutting Out Your Garment

If you would prefer the crew neckline or turtleneck, they are discussed in "Variations."

The square neck raglan included in the Ladies' Raglan Pattern 200 is discussed on the following pages.

Trace one body and one sleeve pattern. After tracing your pattern pieces onto Perky Pattern Paper or Do-Sew, you should also trace the two small pattern pieces marked "Square Neck Adapter." Tape them on the pattern as indicated by the dotted line.

Place the pattern pieces on your fabric with the greater amount of stretch going across the pattern (around the body). If you are matching stripes, be sure they are straight at the underarm, the bottom of the garment, the bottom of the sleeve, and at the neckline. The stripe at the underarm of the body should correspond to the stripe at the underarm of the sleeve. Cut two sleeves and two body pieces which include the square neck adapter. See Fig. 1 for suggested layout.

Construction of Your Garment

SEAMS

Lay the garment pieces on a flat surface and pin one sleeve to one body piece with right sides together. Take care to be certain that you have a sleeve piece _and_ a body piece. Using a straight stitch and 8 to 10 stitches per inch, sew from the underarm up to the neck edge. Leave the needle

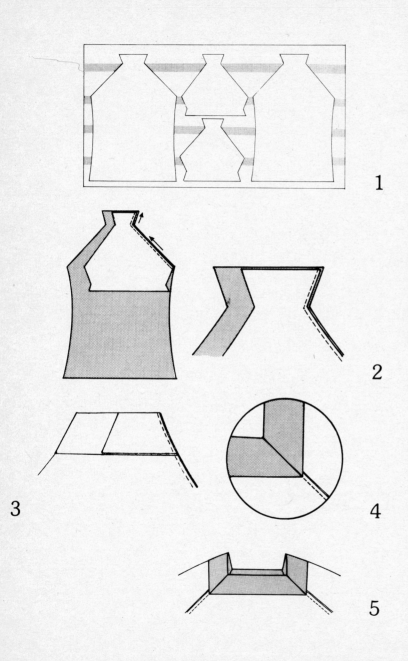

1

2

3

4

5

in the garment, pivot the garment, and sew up to the end of the seam. (Fig. 2)

With right sides together, sew the second sleeve to the same body piece, beginning as before at the underarm and stitching through to the seam edge. Now, stitch the second body piece of the garment to both sleeves, as shown, sewing from the underarm up to the end of the seam.

To enclose the seams at the neck edge of the square neck raglan, fold a set of facings together toward the body of the garment on the fold line indicated on the pattern. Stitch from the fold over the previous stitching line. (Fig. 3) When the garment is opened into the proper position, the seam will fold toward the sleeve and the seam will be enclosed. (Fig. 4) Repeat these directions with the three remaining seams. (Fig. 5)

Sew the side seams using a 1/4-inch seam allowance. Stretch these seams, sewing from the bottom of the garment up through the sleeve edge. (Fig. 6) For a double-strength seam, sew a second row of stitches 1/8 inch from the first stitching line.

HEMS

Try the garment on and mark the length you would like in the sleeve hem and the bottom hem. Press it in and hem as desired by bonding, machine stitching or with a handcatch stitch.

Variations

THE INVISIBLE ZIPPER

This garment is designed to pull comfortably over the head. However, you may wish to insert an invisible zipper into one of the four seams to allow a larger opening. This is particularly convenient for protecting a hairstyle.

You will need a zipper measuring 7 to 9 inches in length or one that is a few inches shorter than the seam into which it will be inserted.

If you do not have a zipper of the correct length and it is necessary to shorten the one you will use, mark the length you need and measure down another 3/4 inch. Using a double thread, handstitch over both rows of zipper teeth. Cut the end off the zipper just below this hand-stitching, taking care to cut <u>between</u> the zipper teeth. (Fig. 7)

On the right side of the fabric, place the opened zipper face down onto the open seam. The head of the zipper should be 1/4 inch below the fold line of the facing, and the edge of the zipper tape should extend slightly beyond the raw edge of the seam in order to keep a 1/4 inch seam allowance consistent throughout the garment. (Fig. 8)

Set your machine on straight stitch and center the needle in the hole of the zipper foot. Place the zipper coil in an upright position in the groove of the zipper foot. Lower the foot and stitch from the top of the zipper until the foot touches the stop of the zipper at the end. Backstitch and clip threads. Test the position of the zipper by closing it. While it is closed, pin the unstitched side of the zipper tape to the right side of the other seam of the garment with the tape positioned exactly as in the previous stitching. (Fig. 9) Pin the top of the zipper to hold it in position and open it again before beginning to stitch.

Sew this second side of the zipper exactly as you did the first side. Backstitch and clip the threads. Close the zipper again and check to be certain that the zipper tape is not visible from the right side of the garment. If some of the tape can

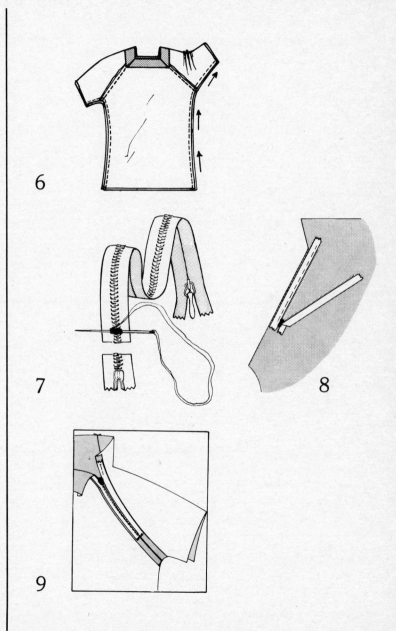

6

7

8

9

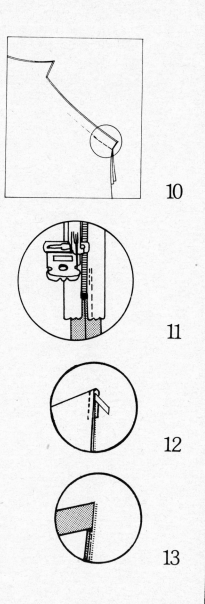

10

11

12

13

be seen, readjust the zipper foot so that the needle is closer to the teeth and re-stitch. It is not necessary to remove your previous stitching.

Slide the zipper foot to the left so the needle passes through the notch. Close the zipper and place the right sides of the fabric together. To complete the seam, align the seam allowances. Insert the needle 1/2 inch from the end of the zipper seam and 1/16 inch to the left of the zipper stitching. Lower the zipper foot and stitch to the end of the garment seam. (Fig. 10) Where you began the seam, pull the bobbin thread through and knot it.

After installation, 1 inch of the zipper will extend below the opening. Slide the foot so the needle is in the outside notch and stitch on each side, as shown, only through the zipper tape and the seam allowance. This extra stitching will help the zipper to lie flat and will also ease the strain which occurs when the zipper is closed. (Fig. 11)

To complete the neck edge at the top of the zipper, sandwich the seam by bringing the facing up and over the top of the zipper and folding the tape into the seam allowance. (Fig. 12) Bring the facing back to the wrong side and the zipper teeth will be exposed. (Fig. 13)

The Invisible Zipper in a Diagonally Striped Fabric or in a Bias Seam

This technique of matching may be used to match a plaid, a diagonal stripe, a border print, a large flower, or other design. The fabric must first be cut so as to ensure that the design will match.

Install the first side of the zipper as above. Close the zipper. Fold back the fabric so that the right side of the zipper and fabric are visible. Fold back the seam allowance of the unstitched side.

Using cellophane tape on the right side of the fabric, align both sides of the garment so that they match.

Turn the fabric to the wrong side and use the tape to attach the unstitched side of the zipper tape to the fabric seam allowance. Remove the tape from the right side of the garment and open the zipper. Stitch the taped side of the zipper and complete the installation of the zipper as above, removing the remaining tape when you have finished.

*The Invisible Zipper in a Plaid
or Striped Fabric*

Sew the first side of the zipper. Close the zipper. Lay the unstitched side of the zipper face down on the outside of the fabric. With a soft-leaded pencil, mark the zipper tape on that side at each instance of a plaid or stripe. Continue with regular invisible zipper installation, matching the pencil markings when stitching on the second side.

RAGLAN SLEEVE TOP WITH CREW, MOCK TURTLE, OR TURTLENECK NECKLINE

After stitching the raglan sleeves and bodies together, refer to Chapter One, "The Pullover Knit Top," for the chart on preparation, ratios, and application of a crew, mock turtle, or turtleneck. The same techniques apply to the raglan sleeve style. Complete the garment as you would for the square neck raglan top.

ZIPPER IN A TURTLENECK

A turtleneck may be applied to many Stretch and Sew patterns. Adding a zipper makes it more comfortable and convenient for many people. The following three methods call for a 12-inch zipper. Whichever method you choose, read the instructions for Finish A. Finishes B and C are variations on this method.

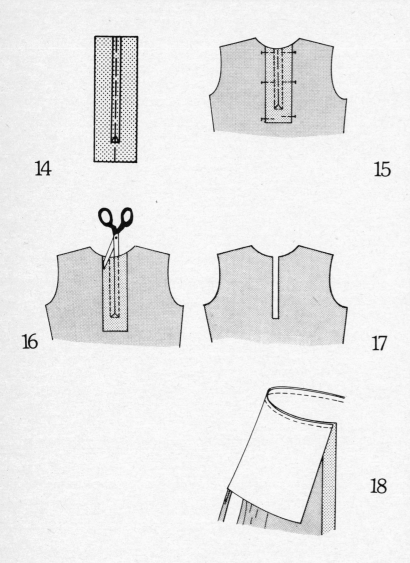

14

15

16

17

18

Finish A

With this method, the zipper will fold down with the turtleneck trim. Cut the turtleneck trim. This trim may be of self-fabric or of rib knit. It should measure 9-1/4 inches wide and 1/2 inch longer than the distance around the total neck opening. If you prefer a snugger turtleneck, you may cut it shorter. This allows a 2-inch finished turtleneck trim with 1/4 inch of ease where the trim folds over the zipper, a 1/4 inch seam allowance at the neck edge, and 3/4 inch for ease in finishing.

From Do-Sew or a light woven fabric stay, cut a 2 inch by 9 inch piece to be used as a stay for the zipper. Draw a box on the stay which measures 8-1/4 inches long and 1/4 inch wide. Use your ruler! Draw a line down the center of the box and a 1/2 inch wedge at the bottom. (Fig. 14)

Mark the center front or center back of the garment and line up the center of the stay with this mark, pinning the stay in place on the right side of the fabric. (Fig. 15)

Stitch with 12 stitches per inch all around the box. Then, clip down the center line and into the corners at the bottom of the box. This will leave a wedge at the bottom. (Fig. 16)

Turn the stay to the wrong side and press. (Fig. 17) Sew the shoulder seams and press them toward the back.

Sew the trim to the neck edge, extending it 1/4 inch beyond the center of the garment and keeping the stay pulled away from the garment. Sew only through <u>one</u> thickness of the turtleneck trim and the garment. Sew with a 1/4 inch seam allowance. (Fig. 18) Press the seam up into the neck trim. (Note: Both ends of the turtleneck will extend 1/4 inch beyond the center front of the garment.)

Place the zipper in position with the metal stop at the end of the zipper in the bottom of the box. The top of the zipper should extend 4 inches onto the turtleneck trim. Lift the garment to expose the wedge, the stay, and the zipper tape. Sew the wedge to the zipper tape and the stay across the bottom of the zipper. (Fig. 19)

Sew the sides of the zipper, folding back the fabric to expose the seam allowance. With the zipper foot, stitch along the seamline. (Fig. 20) At the top of the zipper, fold the ends of the zipper toward the seam allowance. Do not cut them off. (Fig. 21)

Fold the top 4-3/4 inches of the turtleneck trim down, over the top of the zipper to the right side. This will put the right sides of the turtleneck together. To stitch, turn the garment to expose the original stitching line. Stitch again on this line, sewing through the zipper tape and 2 layers of trim. The zipper is sandwiched in between the 2 layers of trim. After stitching, fold the trim into position, exposing the zipper.

The first seam allowance of the turtleneck was pressed up into the trim area. The second seam allowance, after you turn the turtleneck over, should extend toward the garment. Stitch-in-the-ditch at the point where the trim was first sewn onto the neck, sewing from the right side of the garment. Be sure you are catching the seam allowance of the turtleneck in this stitching. (Fig. 22) Trim the excess fabric close to the stitching line.

Finish the garment according to the instructions printed above.

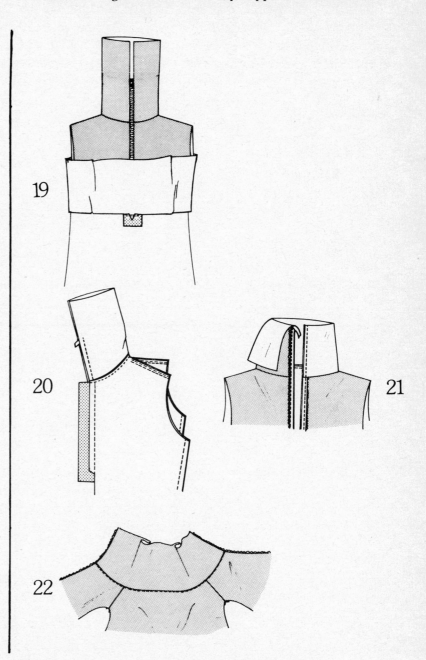

19

20

21

22

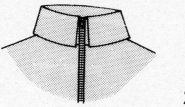

23

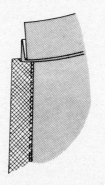

24

Finish B

With this finish, the zipper will extend only to the fold of the turtleneck trim. The turned-down portion of the trim will be unattached. Follow the directions for the zipper which extends all the way up into the turtleneck, but trace a box on the stay which measures 1/4 inch by 10-1/4 inches.

When inserting the zipper into the turtleneck trim, it will extend into the turtleneck 2 inches instead of 4 inches. (Fig. 23) The trim should be folded, right sides together, at the 4 inch marking of the turtleneck trim and stitched in the same manner described for the full zipper in the turtleneck.

Finish the garment according to the instructions printed above.

Finish C

With this method, the zipper will extend to the fold of the turtleneck and the turned-down portion of the trim will be attached along the zipper. Follow the instructions for the full zipper in the turtleneck with these exceptions: Trace a stay which measures 2 inches by 11 inches and draw a box which measures 1/4 inch by 10-1/4 inches.

Continue following instructions for the first variation through Fig. 18. Fold the turtleneck trim, wrong sides together, with a 3/4 inch seam allowance extending below the neck seam. Fold the trim in the finished turtleneck position. Then, fold up the inside section of the turtleneck trim. It is important that this not be included in the first stitching of the zipper. (Fig. 24)

Place the zipper in position with the metal stop at the end of the zipper in the bottom of the box. The top of the zipper should extend onto the folded portion of the turtleneck trim. Lift the garment to expose the wedge, the stay, and the zipper tape. Sew the wedge to the zipper tape and the stay across the bottom of the zipper.

Sew the sides of the zipper, folding back the fabric to expose the seam allowance. With the zipper foot, stitch along the seamline. (Fig. 25) At the top of the zipper, fold the ends of the zipper toward the seam allowance. Do not cut them off.

Fold the top 2-3/4 inches of the turtleneck trim down, over the top of the zipper to the right side. This will put the right sides of the turtleneck together. To stitch, turn the garment to expose the original stitching line. Stitch again on this line, sewing through the zipper tape and the layers of trim. The zipper is sandwiched in between the two layers of trim. (Fig. 26) After stitching, fold the trim into position, exposing the zipper.

The first seam allowance of the turtleneck was pressed up into the trim area. The second seam allowance, after you turn the turtleneck over, should extend into the garment area. Stitch-in-the-ditch at the point where the trim was first sewn onto the neck, sewing from the right side of the garment. Be sure you are catching the seam allowance of the turtleneck in this stitching. (Figs. 27 & 28)

Finish the garment according to the previous instructions.

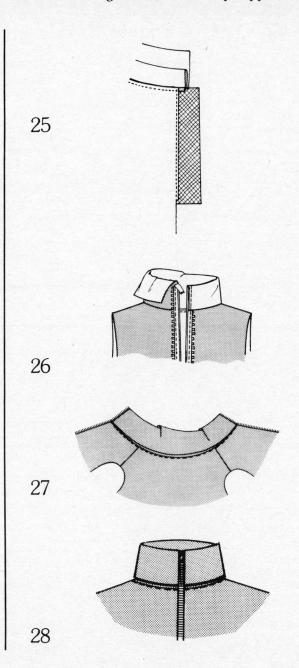

25

26

27

28

5

The Alpaca Cardigan
The Alpaca Pullover
The Cross-Over V-Neckline

Introduction

The first Stretch and Sew class ever taught included instructions for making an alpaca sweater. In those days, the fabric was not as luxurious, and the colors were definitely limited.

Today, there is really no limit to the new colors we can add to our line. In addition, with the use of a computer, we can color-match a wide variety of fabrics, such as men's wear twill, to coordinate exactly with our alpaca fabric. We have also added acrylic to the line of colors which is being knitted in the special alpaca stitch. This makes it possible for those who are unable to wear the wool and alpaca blend to have the same lovely sweaters in dyed-to-match acrylic.

To many people, alpaca is a completely new fabric. Its name is derived from an animal native to the mountains of Peru. Alpaca fabric is a blend, usually of alpaca and wool fibers, which produces a natural fiber product. Stretch and Sew alpaca fabric is a combination blending 50 per cent wool and 50 per cent alpaca. Not only does the yarn dye well, but it also knits up beautifully. It makes a superior garment which, with only a little special attention, stays lovely for many years.

In this chapter, we will cover the traditional "golf sweater" style cardigan as well as the alpaca pullover with the crossed-over V-neckline. You will be especially proud to wear either one with the knit top you created in your first Stretch and Sew class and to combine it with the slacks or a skirt from Chapter Two.

Both sweaters employ the same Stretch and Sew techniques you learned in making the pullover knit top: the neckband and cuffs are stretched to fit the garment; nearly all the seams are stretched as you sew; and the hems are done in the same manner. You will be proud to create a professional looking and attractive alpaca sweater. After making one, you will want to create an enviable alpaca for each member of your family.

The Alpaca Cardigan
The Alpaca Pullover
The Cross-Over V-Neckline

Alpaca is a luxurious knit that, with just a little special care, stays lovely for many years. The term alpaca has also come to mean a special stitch: a purl stitch which is often referred to as a "link" stitch. Since alpaca fibers are very long, they are resistant to pilling. Alpaca fabric also differs from most other knit fabrics because the elasticity, or stretch, is up and down instead of across. For this reason, alpaca sweaters must be cut with the courses (lines of knit stitches) running vertically.

For your fifth Stretch and Sew class, you will need the following items:

Ladies' and Men's Cardigan, Pattern 500/600
Perky Pattern Paper or Do-Sew
Fabric: 1 yard of Stretch & Sew alpaca
*Two yards of rolled edge trim (for the
  cardigan sweater)*
1-1/2 bands of alpaca ribbing
Buttons (for the cardigan sweater)
Sewing aids listed in Chapter One

Preparation of Alpaca Fabric

Before you begin to cut out your garment, the alpaca must be blocked properly to make it easier to work with and to prevent the finished garment from "growing." Remember that, unlike other knit fabrics, alpaca's stretch is up and down, not across.

1. Leave the alpaca fabric in its original tubular shape and soak it with cold water in a basin.

2. Place the wet fabric in the washing machine on the normal spin cycle. This will extract the water but will not harm the fabric. Do not let the fabric agitate in the machine because this could cause it to mat.

3. After the water has been removed, place the alpaca on a smooth surface to block it. Do not put it on towels, as this slows the drying process. A table, or even your floor, covered with a piece of plastic, will serve as a work space for drying and blocking.

4. If you have purchased one yard of fabric, maintain that one yard length when you are blocking the fabric. Do not pull or stretch it out lengthwise. Spread the fabric out gently and slowly by patting it with your hands across the width. (Fig. 1) Keep the rows of stitches straight and the fabric flat and smooth. Don't allow the fabric to ruffle. (Fig. 2) In this way, you can add as much as 10 inches of width to each side of the tube of fabric — a total of 20 inches.

5. Allow the fabric to dry overnight in its original tubular shape.

The stretch that was removed from the fabric was the up and down stretch. Garments of alpaca are cut the horizontal way of the fabric. The horizontal stretch, which will be around the body, has not been eliminated. The process I

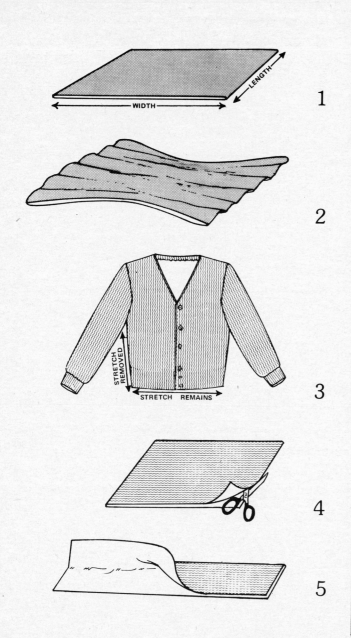

suggest eliminates any chance of your garment "growing" after it has been cut and sewn. (Fig. 3)

Since the rib trim and the rolled edge trim of the sweater have not been pre-treated, I recommend that you have your finished sweater dry cleaned. To maintain the lovely "blouse" of the sleeves and the back, your sweater should be cleaned but <u>not</u> pressed.

I have friends who wash their alpaca sweaters successfully with cold water, using cold water soap. However, if my sweaters get within 12 inches of soap and water, they shrink. So, if you decide you are an expert at hand-washing wool, you may want to try washing your alpaca. The risk is yours. <u>I always dry clean mine.</u> (Do not steam press your alpaca sweater!)

The Alpaca Cardigan

Determining Your Pattern Size

Stretch & Sew Pattern 500/600 is sized according to the bust or chest measurement. Measure the full bust or the fullest part of the chest and choose the pattern of corresponding size. For example, if the measurement is 38 inches, you will select a size 38 pattern. The correct size should be traced from the master pattern onto Perky Pattern Paper or Do-Sew pattern material.

Cutting Out Your Garment

When your fabric has dried, you are ready to begin cutting. Open the tube of alpaca as shown in Fig. 4. Refold the alpaca to create a long narrow strip. The rib lines will be running the length of the strip. (Fig. 5)

The alpaca cardigan has a 2-inch finished rib added to the bottom of the back. The pattern is designed, therefore, with the front 4 inches longer than the back. The front is turned up 2-1/4 inches for a hem. Position the pattern on the fabric. (Fig. 6) <u>Do not cut the ribbing or trim at this time.</u>

You will want to ravel 2 or 3 strands of yarn from the rib trim (not from the sweater). This will be needed to finish the hand stitching on the sweater. Steam press the raveled yarn to uncrinkle it.

6

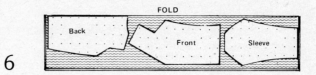

Construction of Your Garment

There is no right or wrong side in alpaca. You will determine a "right side" of your fabric when you sew the shoulder seam. Maintain this throughout construction. Do not, at any stage in construction, use a zigzag or machine overcasting stitch because this could cause the seams to ruffle.

SHOULDER SEAMS

With right sides together, stitch the shoulder seams, using a straight stitch with 9 stitches per inch. <u>Do not stretch these shoulder seams as you sew</u>. The stretch caused by the machine's presser foot on the fabric will be sufficient. Any additional stretching in this area would create a seam which was too long.

There are two techniques for finishing these shoulder seams. One is by hand, using the raveling from the trim. The second method employs machine stitching. Consider, in deciding which to use, how frequently the garment will be worn and how actively it will be used. In addition, consider how important a "professional appearance" is to you in your garment. Machine stitching is rarely used in a finer garment such as a professional's "golf sweater."

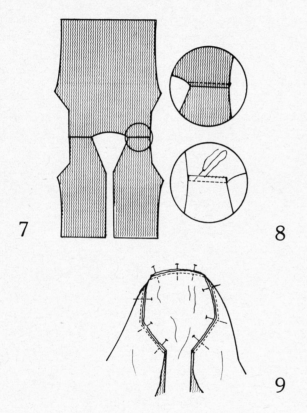

7

8

9

1. Machine finishing: Fold both seam allowances to the back of the sweater. Topstitch on the right side of the garment 3/8 inch from the first row of stitching, through all thicknesses. (Fig. 7) Do <u>not</u> stretch this seam as you sew!

2. Hand-felled seam finishing: With both seam allowances pressed to the back, trim the under seam allowance to 3/8 inch. Fold the top seam allowance over and under the 3/8-inch seam allowance. (Fig. 8) With a small slip stitch, using a single strand of the raveled alpaca yarn from the trim, sew the folded edge of the seam down.

Seam tape will not be necessary because either of the above seam finishes will provide sufficient support. In fact, seam tape would tend to create too much rigidity in the shoulder seam.

SLEEVES

Check the seam allowance in your pattern before beginning to sew. Mark the center of the sleeve with a pin. There is no right or wrong side to alpaca so you may use either side of the fabric as the right side. Pin the sleeve to the shoulder seam, matching the dot markings on the sleeve and the garment. (Fig. 9) Using a straight stitch and slightly stretching as you sew, with the garment body on top and the sleeve next to the machine, sew the sleeve to the garment. Sufficient stretching is usually accomplished by pulling slightly from the front as the fabric is fed through the machine.

From the wrong side of the garment, lightly steam the seam allowance out into the sleeve.

RIB TRIM

With the right side up, place the back of the sweater on a flat surface. Measure the width across the bottom. Use a ratio of 3:4 in measuring out your rib trim. This means that for every 4 inches of sweater, you should use 3 inches of trim. Therefore, if the bottom edge of your sweater back measures 15 inches, it will require a 12-inch strip of trim. You may use purchased trim to match or self-fabric trim which has been cut with the stretch of the fabric strip going lengthwise. Your trim should be 4-1/2 inches wide. If it is wider, you should carefully ravel it back from the unfinished edge to the correct width. When folded lengthwise, the trim will measure 2-1/4 inches wide. (Fig. 10)

As you did when constructing the pullover knit top, divide the sweater back and the rib trim into fourths. With the right sides together and the open edges of the trim even with the cut edge of the sweater, match the quarter divisions. (Fig. 11) Using a 1/4-inch seam, stretch the trim to equal the sweater width as you sew. Do <u>not</u> press this seam.

SIDE SEAMS

Match the underarm and side seams, leaving the 2-1/4 inch hem allowance at the side fronts extending below the sweater back. (Fig. 12) Using a straight stitch and stretching slightly as you sew, stitch the side seams, beginning at the bottom of the garment and stitching up the side, out to the end of the sleeve. (Fig. 12)

HEM

Fold the front hem up and over the back trim at the side seam. (Fig. 13) Pin it into place. Turn the sweater over and stitch, from the bottom up, over the first side seam, catching the hem.

Unfold the hem and re-fold it into place on the sweater front. This will enclose the seam. (Fig. 14) Press the hem into place and sew it with a raveling from the rib trim, which you prepared earlier. Use a handcatch stitch over the raw edge.

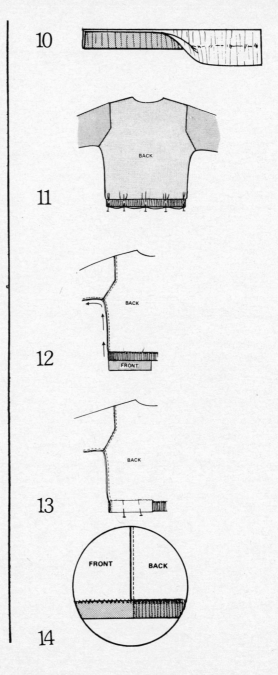

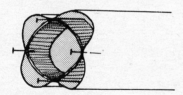

15

CUFFS

Before sewing the cuff onto the sleeve, it is necessary to make certain that the sleeve is the correct length. Take the following two measurements, which should be equal: 1) The distance from the shoulder bone to the wrist bone. 2) The distance on the garment sleeve from the shoulder seam to the wrist edge. Make any necessary adjustments. When the cuff is attached, it will bring the sleeve up slightly, giving a bloused effect.

From a piece of rib trim 4-1/2 inches wide, cut a 6- to 7-inch length for each cuff (6 inches for a lady and 7 inches for a man). A strip of self trim may be used here as well as for the trim at the bottom of the sweater back.

Sew the cuff ends together to form a cylinder. Finger press the seam open and fold the cuff in half to create a cylinder which is 2-1/4 inches wide. Divide the cuff and the sleeve edge into fourths and pin the two together, matching these divisions. (Fig. 15)

Because the sleeve opening is very large and the cuff is small, care must be taken to attach the two evenly: Place the first quarter division under the presser foot of the machine. Remove the marking pin and insert the needle through the cuff and into the sleeve. Stretch the first division of the cuff as far as it will allow. With the rib stretched and held against the sweater fabric, slip your fingers under the rib from the folded edge. Carefully pull the edge of the sleeve back to meet the cut edge of the rib trim. As the sleeve is pulled back, the fabric will ease into the cuff. This will enable you to sew across each quarter division.

For each quarter division, repeat this technique, holding the rib in your right hand. Use your left hand to bring the sweater edge into place, adjusting the fullness. Turn the sleeve to the right side. Do not press because this would eliminate the softly bloused effect you have created.

ROLLED EDGE TRIM

Two yards of rolled edge trim will be sufficient for a lady's or man's sweater. Rolled edge trim has very little stretch so that the usual rule for applying the trim to knits is reversed: <u>Make the sweater fit the trim, not the trim fit the sweater.</u>

The trim will be applied with a 1:1 ratio. Lay the trim on the <u>pattern</u> and measure the amount needed:

1. Leaving 1/2 inch of trim extending below the hemline, begin measuring at the bottom of the pattern up through to the point of the V. (Fig. 16)

2. Mark this distance on your strip of trim with chalk or pins.

3. Pivot and measure to the shoulder seam. Mark the trim.

4. Measure the back of the neck from shoulder seam to shoulder seam.

5. Mark the trim in this area 1 inch smaller than your measurement as the sweater will be eased when you apply the trim to the neck.

Rolled edge trim has a permanent curl on one side. Place the trim with the curl face down on the right side of the sweater and the curled edge approximately 1/2 inch in from the edge. The trim will be on top of the sweater when you apply it.

16

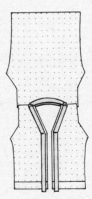

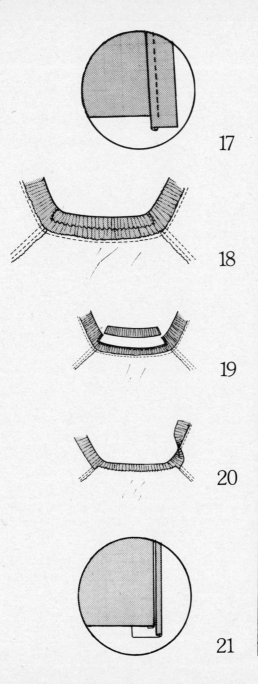

17

18

19

20

21

Start at the bottom, using your zipper foot, and sew just behind the roll of the trim. It is important that the front of the sweater is in a relaxed position, and the trim is not being stretched as it is sewn to the front of the sweater. (Fig. 17)

Sew up the front of the sweater, leaving the needle in the fabric at the point of the V, and raise the sewing machine foot. Swing the sweater around so that it is again lined up straight on your machine. Let the presser foot down. The trim will go around this corner without a miter.

Since you are sewing with the rolled trim on top of the machine, you should have no difficulty easing the sweater in and making it fit the trim in the neck area.

To create the curve at the back of the sweater neck, mark and zigzag stitch a cutting line on the trim at the neck, which is one-half the width of the trim, from one shoulder seam to the other. (Fig. 18) Trim away this part of the neck trim. (Fig. 19) Now, whipstitch the trim to the back of the sweater neck and to the shoulder seams. (Fig. 20)

Now, fold the trim to the wrong side of the sweater. The rolled edge will roll toward the sweater, and the trim, as shown, will lie flat on the underside. (Fig. 21)

Turn the 1/2-inch seam allowance of the trim, which is at the bottom of the sweater, to the inside. Now, fold the rolled edge trim over it, into a finished position. (Fig. 22) Hand tack it in place.

BUTTONHOLES

Before beginning, remember that ladies' sweaters button right over left, and men's are buttoned left over right! An alpaca cardigan generally has 5 buttons up the front. The top button is placed at the point of the V; the bottom button at the center of the hem; and the other three spaced evenly between.

A looser zigzag stitch is best for buttonholes on sweater knits. Make vertical, machine-stitched buttonholes, sewing on the <u>trim</u> side.

The Alpaca Pullover

From the same pattern you may make a sporty pullover sweater as comfortable and as fun to wear as your cardigan. Prepare the fabric, as you did the cardigan, by blocking and re-folding it before cutting out the garment.

Cutting Out Your Garment

Use <u>only</u> the back and the sleeve pieces of your pattern. Place the pattern on the fabric so that the greater amount of stretch is going across the pattern (around the body).

Cut the body of the sweater on the top line of the pattern, which is marked "cut here for the back, add ribbing here." One of the backs which you cut will become the front. You will need two sleeves and two body pieces. (Fig. 23)

The depth of the "V" which you will cut on the garment depends upon who will wear it and will vary slightly with the size of the garment. The general rule is: 8 inches for a man's sweater, 7 inches for a lady's sweater, and 6 inches for a child's garment. This measurement is taken down the center front fold.

To cut the desired "V" in the garment front, fold the front in half and cut the V, beginning at its point and cutting up to the neck edge of the shoulder seam. (Fig. 24)

22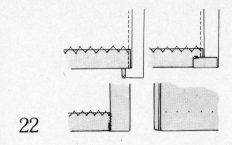

23

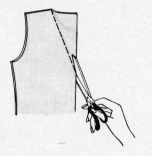

24

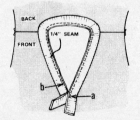

25

Construction of Your Garment

SHOULDER SEAMS

Check the seam allowances each time you begin to sew. With the right sides together, stitch the shoulder seams, using a straight stitch with 9 stitches per inch. Do not stretch this seam! The stretch caused by the sewing machine presser foot will be sufficient.

THE CROSS-OVER V-NECKLINE

Using a strip of self-trim at the neck edge of the garment, you will enjoy making an attractive "cross-over V-neckline." This is particularly helpful in a child's garment, for it allows a comfortable fit over their proportionally large heads. It also lends a sporty look to any sweater. While the ratios in this section are only for sweater knits, this neckline finish can be adapted to other knit fabrics as described in "Variations" at the end of the chapter.

You will need a strip of alpaca fabric 2-1/2 inches wide and 1 to 2 inches longer than the length of the neck opening. Cut this strip of self-fabric trim so that the greater amount of stretch follows the length of the neckband piece. Fold the neckband in half the long way. Place the neckband on the neck edge of the garment with the cut edges even. (Fig. 25) Leave at least a 1-inch extension of the neckband at each side of the V-point to be crossed over.

Beginning directly under the V, at the center point (Fig. 25a), stitch up toward the shoulder area. Use a 1/4-inch seam and use a stretch ratio of 3:4. As you approach the back of the neck, increase your stretch to a ratio of at least 2:3. As you finish the shoulder curve and come down to the opposite side of the V-neck, decrease the stretch again to a ratio of 3:4. Stop stitching

1-1/2 inches from the point where you began stitching. (Fig. 25b)

Remove the garment from the machine and turn it inside out. Clip the center front of the garment down to the point where the stitching begins. (Fig. 26) Clip through the garment only, not through the trim. This clipping releases the fabric, allowing you to bring the trim up into position.

Turn the garment right side out and tuck the width of the unsewn trim into the front of the garment at the area which was left unsewn. (Fig. 27) Cross the remaining piece of neck trim <u>under</u> the first piece. (Fig. 28) Place the garment on a flat surface to arrange the crossed-over area in its proper position. Pin it into place through all thicknesses of the trim.

With the trim in the finished position, lift the front of the garment until the unstitched part of the trim is exposed. Stitch from the point of the V, <u>along the seam allowance</u>, up to meet the previous stitching. (Fig. 29) Fasten the loose tab on the opposite side to the seam allowance.

SLEEVES AND CUFFS

Follow the instructions for the cardigan to attach the sleeves and cuffs.

SIDE SEAMS

Match the underarm and side seams. Using a straight stitch and stretching slightly as you sew, stitch from the bottom of the garment, up the side, and out the sleeve seam to the wrist edge.

WAIST EDGE TRIM

The last step to complete this beautiful sweater is to add the rib trim to the bottom of the pullover. Measure the person's body where you want the sweater rib to be, holding the tape

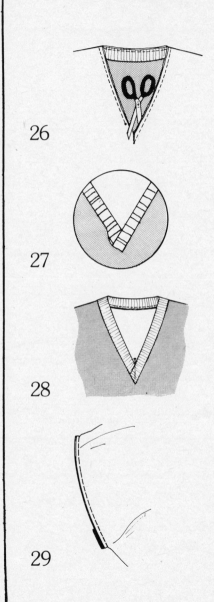

26

27

28

29

taut but not tight. Use approximately 1 inch less rib knit trim than this measurement, plus 1/2 inch for seam allowances. For example, your finished rib should be 33-1/2 inches for a hip measurement of 34 inches. Or, you may cut your rib to equal 3/4 the distance around the bottom of your sweater plus 1/2 inch.

Sew your trim in a cylinder, using a 1/4-inch seam. Finger press the seam open and fold the rib trim in half, lengthwise, forming a cylinder. Divide the garment and trim in fourths, marking with pins or chalk. Match the 4 division marks and pin the trim in place. The cut edge of the trim is placed against the cut edge of the garment, right sides together. Stitch with a 1/4-inch seam allowance, using a straight stitch.

Variations

THE CROSS-OVER V WITH NONSWEATER FABRIC

Any appropriate Stretch and Sew Pattern can be used. If a lower neck is preferred or if this garment is to be worn over another garment, cut away 3/4 to 1 inch from the neck edge. Cut the V by measuring down the center front fold the desired V depth. With Pattern 500/600, you use the pattern back for your front. But when you are measuring down from a front neck edge, the average V depth is 4 inches for a child, 5 inches for a woman, and 6 inches for a man.

With rib trim or trim from fabric with 50 per cent or more stretch, stretch the trim only slightly from the point of the V to the shoulder. Stretch it across the back of the neck from shoulder seam to shoulder seam with a 2:3 ratio. With trim from fabric with less than 50 per cent stretch, sew from the point of the V to the shoulder, using a 1:1 ratio. Stretch across the back of the neck from shoulder seam to shoulder seam with a 3:4 ratio.

6

The Tab Front Knit Top
The Welt Pocket

Introduction

The technique we have developed, a fool-proof method of sewing a tab front, is as delightful in a very dressy garment as it is in the sportier version.

The tab front is really a placket opening. It is wonderful for little boys' and girls' knit tops. Dads love them for golf. And the ladies use them everywhere — from the length drawn in the pattern to the long, extended-to-the-waist tabs in sport tops and street dresses, or even extended to the knee for evening wear. We have used this tab front technique in elegant metallic knits, sportswear fabrics, beautiful silk-like Qiana, and, of course, the wool or polyester double knits so much in use — all with beautiful results.

A coordinating fabric in a different texture or color for the tab front and collar is a lovely fashion detail. Using a plain, coordinating fabric is an especially wise choice in a garment of rib-type fabric because ribs do not lend themselves as well to a tab front. A sharp contrast such as black on white or lime on navy adds a crisp look to a garment.

I have enjoyed using a solid interlock with a striped single knit. If I wish to use a striped fabric for the garment and tab, I cut the tab stripe the opposite direction of the garment line. A bias cut is also excellent.

In this lesson, the welt pocket is also introduced. We have added this easy-to-do pocket technique here because the principles of applying the welt pocket are so similar to the tab front that we believe by combining these two techniques in one lesson, they will have more meaning for you. Once learned, this fashion detail will become a beautiful addition to your wardrobe.

The Tab Front Knit Top
The Welt Pocket

The versatile Ladies' Knit Top with Cap Sleeves Pattern contains three neckline variations: the tab front neck opening with a shirt-type collar, which we will be discussing, plus a funnel neckline and a boat neckline. The tab front facing and collar from this pattern may be adapted to the neckline of any other ladies' pattern.

For your sixth Stretch and Sew class, you will need:

Ladies' Knit Top with Cap Sleeves, Pattern 250
Men's Knit Top, Pattern 1750
Boys' and Girls' Tab Front, Pattern 880 and 890
Perky Pattern Paper or Do-Sew
Do-Sew for stay
Fabric: Single and double knits. The tab facing fabric should not be very much heavier or lighter than the garment. (Refer to pattern envelopes for appropriate yardage.)
Perky Bond Plus interfacing (optional)
Perky Bond, 1 inch wide
Buttons (optional)
Sewing aids listed in Chapter One

The Tab Front

Determining Your Pattern Size

The Stretch and Sew Patterns 250 and 1750 are sized according to the bust or chest measurement. Measure the full bust or the fullest part of the chest and trace off the corresponding size pattern from your master pattern to Perky Paper or Do-Sew pattern material.

mans left over right
ladies right over left

stay stitching

1

2

Cutting Out Your Garment

Place the pattern on your fabric so that the greater stretch in the fabric goes across the pattern (around the body).

Construction of Your Garment

TAB FRONT STAY

Transfer the stitching and cutting lines from the pattern to your tab front stay fabric. Do-Sew pattern material makes an excellent stay. Indicate the center front of your garment by using pins or tailor tacks or by pressing.

Pin the stay to the wrong side of the garment front at the center front neck edge. Be certain the center line of the stay is exactly on the center front line of the garment. Sew 12 stitches per inch along the stitching line indicated on the pattern, forming a box. (Fig. 1) Cut on the cutting lines inside the box. Cut to the point of the wedge but do not cut on the diagonal lines extending into the corners. (Fig. 2)

TAB FRONT FACINGS

If you are planning to use either bound or machine-stitched buttonholes in your garment, a reinforcement strip is necessary. Cut a strip of bonding material (Perky Bond Plus) 1-1/2 inches wide and the length of the tab. Bond it to the wrong side of the facing from the fold line out toward the facing. (Fig. 3)

Place the tab front facings on the front of the garment, right sides together. The straight edges of the facings should be even with the cut edges inside the box. Pin the facings in place with the heads of the pins extending into the open box. (Fig. 4)

[handwritten: Basting]

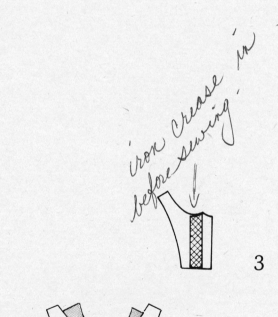

[handwritten: iron crease in before sewing]

3

4

With the garment on top and the facings on the bottom, stitch the facings to the fronts exactly along the stitching lines. Backstitch at the ends of both stitching lines to secure stitches. Do not stitch across the bottom of the box at this time. (Fig. 5)

Cut on the diagonal lines to the stitching line in the box corners, forming a wedge. Cut through the stay and the front seam allowance. (Fig. 6) Press the seam allowances toward the garment.

Determine if this tab will fold left over right (for men) or right over left (for women). The way the tab folds over will determine which tab to position first.

To position the top facing in the opening, tuck both facings to the wrong side. Then, fold the top facing on the fold line to exactly meet the edge of the box. (Fig. 7) Tuck the wedge at the bottom of the box down into the wrong side of the garment. Lift the stay and the bottom edge of the garment up out of the way and machine-baste across the wedge. One tab facing will be included in this stitching. (Fig. 8)

Fold the bottom facing on the fold line. Place it under the top and carefully press. Lift the garment front and stay, stitching through the wedge and both facings. (Fig. 9) Press the tab area carefully. (Fig. 10)

SHOULDER SLEEVE SEAMS

Sew the shoulder seams with right sides together from the neck edge to the sleeve edge. Press the seams open.

COLLAR

If your fabric needs more stability in the collar, cut interfacing (Perky Bond Plus) for the under or upper collar. For a more stable collar, both sides can be bonded. Bond according to the

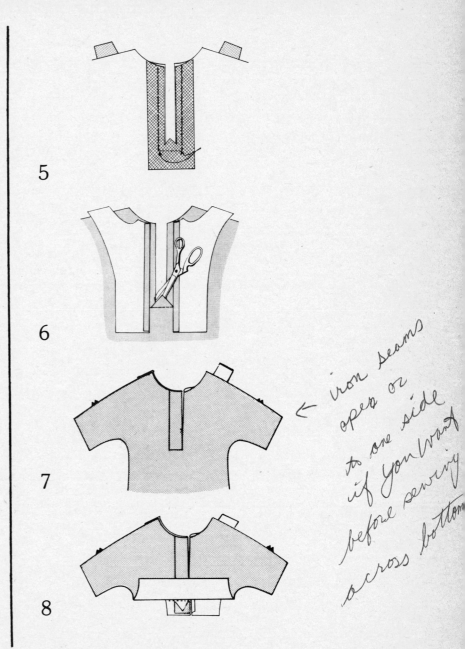

5

6

7

8

← iron seams open or to one side if you want before sewing across bottom

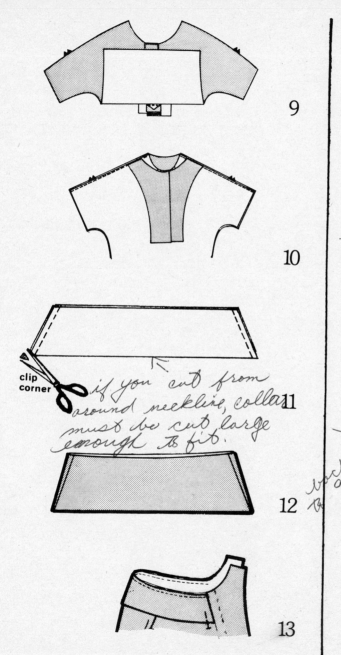

9

10

clip
corner

*if you cut from
around neckline, collar
must be cut large
enough to fit.*

11

*back
9 stitches now
½"*

12

13

bonding instructions found in Basic Principles. Then, fold the collar in half lengthwise, right sides together. Sew the seams along the short ends. Clip diagonally across the corners on the pointed collar. (Fig. 11) Grade the seam if you are using a bulky fabric.

Turn the collar right side out and press with a steam iron and damp cloth. Allow the seams to roll slightly to the underside of the collar as you press. (Fig. 12) *underside - from each side toward over - iron from center toward sides - center*

Pin the center back of the collar to the right side of the center back of the knit top. Pin the ends of the collar to the center fronts of the garment, 3/4 inch in from the fold line of the facings.

Machine baste the collar to the neck edge by sewing from the center front to the center back. At the center back, remove the garment from your machine and begin at the second center front, sewing to meet the first basting at the center back. (Note: The inner tab front facing piece should hang free.) (Fig. 13)

Fold the facing to the right side, matching the seam allowances. Make sure the collar is 3/4 inch in from the front edge fold on both the right and left tabs. (Fig. 14)

Sew the entire neck edge through all thicknesses once again, this time including the facings, beginning at both front edges and sewing to the center back. (Fig. 15)

Trim the seam allowances at the neck edge by grading the lower raw edges and leaving the upper edge untrimmed. (Fig. 16)

Turn the facing back to the inside of the garment and press carefully. Zigzag the back neck seam allowance from shoulder seam to shoulder seam. (Fig. 17)

SIDE SEAMS

Sew with right sides together, stitching from the bottom of the garment up through the underarm area and out to the edge of the sleeve. Stretch as you sew, especially in the underarm area. For extra strength, stitch the seam a second time 1/8 inch from the first stitching. Trim the seam allowance to 1/4 inch in the underarm area. (Fig. 18)

HEM

Press a 1-1/2-inch hem allowance at the bottom of the garment and a 1-inch hem in the sleeves. Finish the hem by bonding, machine-stitching, or with a handcatch stitch.

BUTTONHOLES

Make buttonholes in the top tab and sew buttons on the bottom tab. You may use a button and loop or sew a snap at the upper corner of the tab if you plan to wear the neckline closed to the collar.

Variations

FUNNEL NECK AND BOAT NECK

Pattern 250 includes two other neck variations: the funnel neckline and the boat neckline. Both are very attractive neckline variations, and offer wardrobe variety for this knit top. Complete instructions for cutting and construction are included with the pattern. (Fig. 19)

TAB FRONT USING PERKY BOND PLUS

A quick trick technique for the tab front is to cut the stay from Perky Bond Plus. Transfer the stitching lines and the cutting lines from the pattern to the non-adhesive side of the Perky Bond Plus.

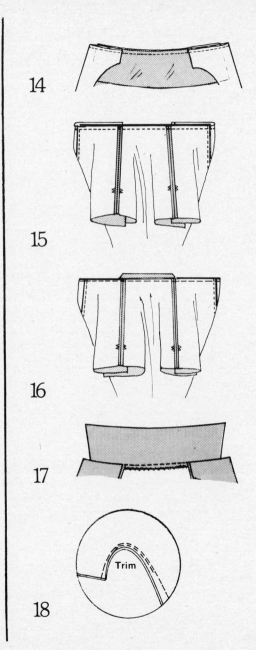

14

15

16

17

18

Trim

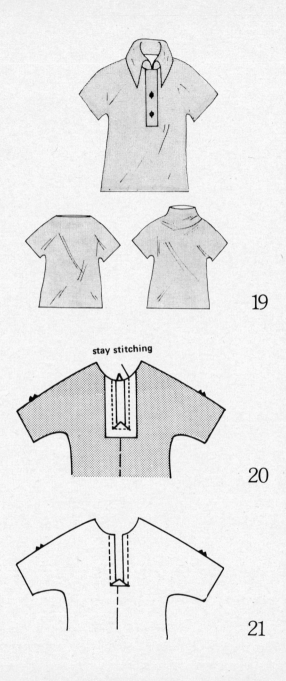

19

stay stitching

20

21

Position the Perky Bond Plus stay on the front of the garment, the adhesive side of the Perky Bond Plus against the right side of the garment. Sew with 12 stitches to the inch along the stitching line indicated on the pattern. (Fig. 20)

Cut on the cutting lines inside the box to the point of the wedge and diagonally into the corners. (Fig. 21) Turn the Perky Bond Plus stay to the wrong side of the garment. Finger press it carefully into place. Do not use an iron on your garment at this time. (Fig. 22)

Fold each facing piece, wrong sides together, on the fold line as marked on the pattern. Press along the fold line. (Fig. 23)

Place the top tab facing over the bottom tab facing. The top facing should lap 1-1/2 inches over the bottom facing. (Fig. 24) Pin these facings together down the center.

Position the garment on the ironing board, right side of the garment up. Place the facings under the tab opening with the top tab exactly filling the box. The folded edge of the tab should be even with the side of the box. Match the front neck edge of the garment and the tabs.

To hold the tabs in place, put pins in the garment at a slight angle along the box seam line. Pin through the garment, the Perky Bond Plus, the tab facings, and into the ironing board pad. (Fig. 25)

Fold back the garment fabric to expose the wedge at the bottom of the box. Press, using a damp cloth and a hot iron (cotton setting) to bond the Perky Bond Plus to the wedge and facing. (Only one-half of each facing and the wedge will be bonded because of the layers of the facing fabric. This area will be stitched later to include all layers.) (Fig. 26)

Fold back the garment front to expose the side seam of the box. Place a piece of paper on the top of the facing piece, sliding the paper under the Perky Bond Plus and the seam allowance along the side of the box. Press the Perky Bond Plus to the seam allowances on the facing and the garment. Use a hot steam iron (cotton setting) and a damp pressing cloth to bond. Repeat on the opposite side.

Trim away the Perky Bond Plus and the paper which have been bonded together. Lift the garment fabric to expose the wedge. Stitch across the wedge of the box, stitching through the wedge, the Perky Bond Plus, and the folded facings.

Fold back the garment fabric to expose the side seam of the box. Stitch through the bonded seam allowance of the garment and the bonded seam allowance of the facing edge. Be sure the Perky Bond Plus stay is completely caught in this seam to prevent it from showing on the right side of the tab. Repeat the same steps on the opposite side.

Complete the knit top from the previous instructions for the tab front, starting at the section labeled "Shoulder Seams."

The Welt Pocket

Welt Pocket with Stay Fabric

To make a welt pocket in a garment, first determine where you want the top of the pocket positioned. Mark a straight line on the garment to indicate the top line of the pocket.

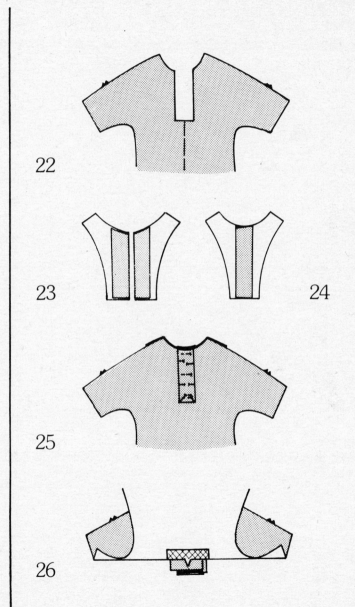

22

23   24

25

26

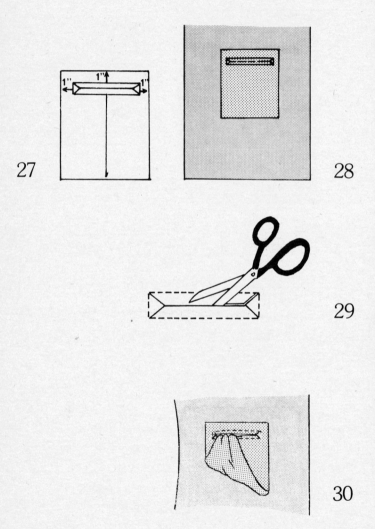

27

28

29

30

CUTTING

From the pocket lining fabric, cut a pocket stay the size of the finished pocket plus 1-inch seam allowances. Draw a box the finished size of the pocket opening with at least 1 inch of the stay above the box and 1 inch on each side. Draw a cutting line along the center of the box and draw wedges at least 1/2 inch long at each end of the box. (Fig. 27)

CONSTRUCTION

Position the pocket stay on the right side of the garment. Match the top line of the box to the line you have drawn on your garment indicating the top of the pocket. Pin it into place. Sew around the box, sewing on the stay fabric, using 12 stitches to the inch. Pivot carefully at each corner. Be sure the stitches overlap where you begin and end sewing so there is no chance that these stitches will pull out. (Fig. 28)

Cut down the center of the box, through the garment and the stay, on the stay's cutting line and clip into the corners forming a wedge at each end of the box. Clip sharply into the corners, being careful not to cut the stitches. (Fig. 29)

Turn the stay to the inside of the garment, through the box. (Fig. 30) Press the stay with your steam iron, making sure none of the stay fabric shows from the right side of the garment.

The pocket is made in one continuous strip, as wide as the pocket opening plus 2 inches and. twice the depth of the finished pocket plus 2 inches. You may apply Perky Bond Plus to the wrong side of the pocket for extra reinforcement if you like.

To form the pocket welt, fold one end of the pocket down 1 inch, wrong sides together. A strip of Perky Bond positioned under the folded end will enable you to work with the pocket welt more easily. (Fig. 31)

Position the welt behind the pocket opening, with the welt completely filling the box and the folded edge of the welt even with the top of the box. A tip here is to position the welt with transparent tape instead of pins since there will be less chance of it slipping out of position. (Fig. 32)

Fold back the garment fabric to expose the wedge at the end of the box. Stitch across the end, sewing through the wedge, the pocket stay, and the welt. Sew the other end to correspond to the first side. Sew from the bottom up to the fold. (Fig. 33)

Fold up the bottom of the garment, exposing the seam at the lower edge of the box. Stitch the seam at the lower edge of the box, sewing through the seam allowance, the pocket stay, and the welt. (Fig. 34)

Position the cut end of the pocket so that it extends up beyond the pocket welt. Press the pocket carefully into position. (Fig. 35) Fold the garment down and stitch the upper seam of the box in the same manner, catching both layers of the pocket. (Fig. 36)

Using a straight stitch, sew all the way around the pocket, rounding the lower corners to prevent lint from collecting. For a second stitching, I like to use a multiple zigzag stitch in this area. However, a zigzag stitch would work, or two rows of straight stitching. Press the pocket area carefully. (Fig. 37)

After the pocket is completed, sew the garment, following the directions that are included with the pattern.

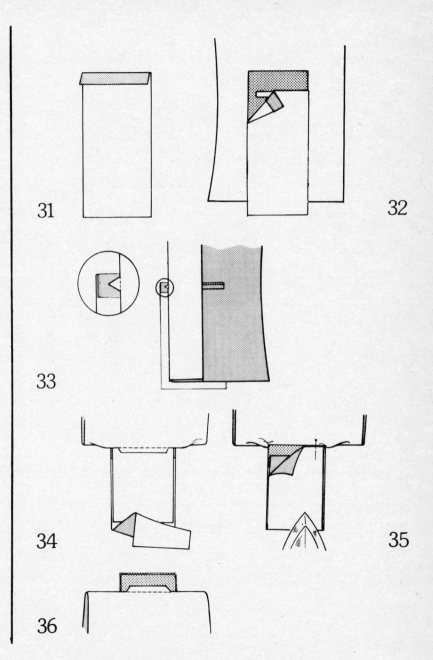

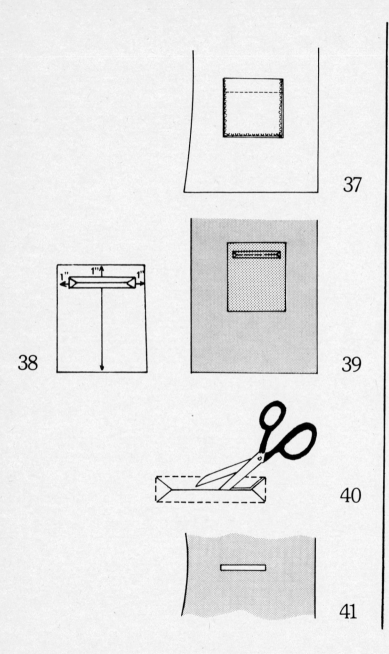

37

38

39

40

41

Welt Pocket with Perky Bond Plus

To make a welt pocket in a garment, first determine where you want the top of the pocket positioned. Mark a straight line on the garment to indicate the top line of the pocket.

CUTTING

From Perky Bond Plus, cut a pocket stay the size of the finished pocket plus 1-inch seam allowances. On the non-adhesive side of the Perky Bond Plus, draw a box the finished size of the pocket opening with at least 1 inch above the box and 1 inch on each side. Draw a cutting line along the center of the box and draw wedges at least 1/2 inch long at each end of the box. (Fig. 38)

CONSTRUCTION

Position the pocket stay on the garment, adhesive side of the Perky Bond Plus against the right side of the garment, matching the top line of the box to the top of the pocket. Pin it into place. If you want matching pockets, sew them both at the same time. Sew around the box, sewing on the stay fabric, using 12 stitches to the inch. Pivot carefully at each corner. Be sure that stitches overlap where you begin and end sewing so there is no chance these stitches will pull out. (Fig. 39)

Cut down the center of the box, through the garment and the stay, on the stay's cutting line, and clip into the corners, forming a wedge at each end of the box. Clip sharply into the corners, being careful not to cut the stitches. (Fig. 40)

Turn the stay to the inside of the garment, through the box. (Fig. 41) Finger press so the Perky Bond Plus does not show on the outside of the garment.

The pocket is made in one continuous strip, as wide as the pocket opening plus 2 inches, and twice the depth of the finished pocket plus 2 inches.

To form the pocket welt, fold down one end of the pocket 1 inch, wrong sides together. (Fig. 42) A strip of Perky Bond positioned under the folded end and bonded will enable you to work with the pocket more easily.

Position the garment on the ironing board, right side of the garment up. Place the welt behind the pocket opening, with the welt completely filling the box and the folded edge of the welt even with the top of the box. To hold the welt in place, put pins in the garment at a slight angle just below the pocket opening, through the garment, the Perky Bond Plus, the pocket and into the ironing board pad. (Fig. 43)

Fold back the garment fabric to expose the wedge at the end of the box. Press, using a damp pressing cloth and a hot steam iron (cotton setting) to bond the wedge to the pocket fabric. Press the wedge at the other end in the same manner. (Fig. 44) Next, press the seam at the lower edge of the box in the same manner as the wedges were pressed, by folding up the garment fabric first to expose the seam and, then, pressing it into place. Continue pressing the entire lower portion of the Perky Bond Plus stay, bonding it to the pocket fabric. (Fig. 45)

Stitch across both ends, sewing through the wedge, the pocket stay, and the welt. Then, stitch the seam at the lower edge of the box in the same manner as the wedges, sewing through the seam allowance, pocket stay, and welt. Make sure the lower portion of the pocket fabric extends down and is not included in this stitching.

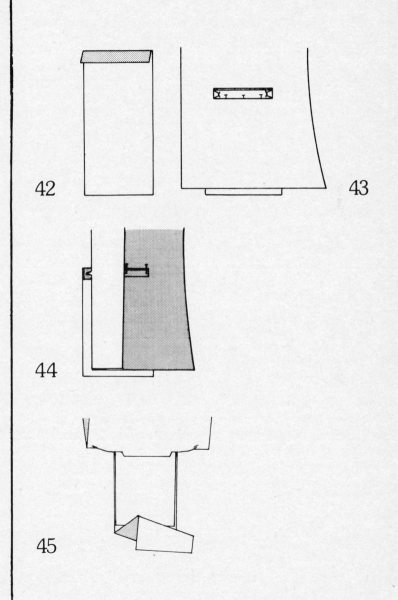

42 43

44

45

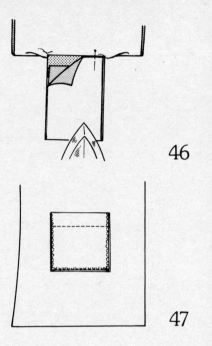

46

47

Position the cut end of the pocket so that it extends up beyond the pocket welt, matching the end of the pocket even with the cut edge of the Perky Bond Plus.

Fold back the garment fabric to expose the seam allowance. Again, using a damp pressing cloth and a hot steam iron, press it into place. (Fig. 46) Stitch across the upper seam of the box, sewing through the seam allowance, the Perky Bond Plus stay and the pocket fabric.

Press the pocket, creasing the fold at the bottom. Using a straight stitch, sew all the way around the pocket, rounding the lower corners to prevent lint from collecting. For a second stitching, I like to use a multiple zigzag stitch in this area. However, a zigzag stitch or two rows of straight stitching would work fine. Press the pocket area carefully. (Fig. 47)

After the pocket is completed, sew the garment, following the directions that are included with the pattern.

7

Ladies' Suit Jacket
Bound Buttonholes
Ladies' Gored Skirts

Introduction

Fashion has an interesting way of repeating itself. Whenever I think I have come up with a really original idea, I realize the garment is something that was done long ago. The two jackets described in Chapter Seven are simple in their design and are, in my opinion, classics. The basic techniques that you will use in the construction of these garments are techniques that will be important to you in many similar, and perhaps more seasonal fashion garments.

Our Kimono Sleeve Jacket, Pattern 1000, lends itself to a knit fabric with grace and elegance. Fabric with both vertical and horizontal stretch is important when making this garment. For this reason, I especially enjoy using a wool double knit.

Our Set-In Sleeve Jacket, Pattern 1050, is another classic garment. A totally new effect can be achieved by just varying the collar slightly and adding a belt. The length may range from a fairly short jacket to a floor length coat.

In addition to jackets, gored skirts are introduced in this chapter. You will enjoy learning to make them, and adding them to your versatile knit wardrobe will be a pleasure. The Multi-Gored Skirt, Pattern 425, is drawn in street length. With the use of a yardstick, each gore may be extended and a beautiful hostess skirt will be the result. Another version of the same pattern is the flip skirt. Simple, comfortable, and stylish, the technique for sewing the hem in this skirt is one that I feel sure you will enjoy learning and will find valuable many times in the future when you are working with a curved hem.

We have advanced in this Stretch and Sew lesson to a more tailored garment than previously. Consequently, pressing is a key factor. Each seam should be pressed with the aid of a damp cloth as it is sewn. Pressing will tell the story. Are you doing a professional job or do your garments say "homemade"? Avoid over-pressing embossed stitches as this can be as much a sign of lack of sewing skill as an underpressed garment. A damp cloth, a good warm iron creating plenty of steam, and a light hand is the secret. And, of course, you must press as you sew.

Ladies' Suit Jacket
Bound Buttonholes
Ladies' Gored Skirts

For your seventh Stretch and Sew class, you will need:

Ladies' Set-In Sleeve Jacket, Pattern 1050
Ladies' Kimono Sleeve Jacket, Pattern 1000
Ladies' Gored Skirts, Pattern 425
Perky Pattern Paper or Do-Sew
Fabric: Wool double knit, polyester, wool and
*   polyester blends, cotton double knit,*
*   acrylics, deerskin and fun fur. (Refer to*
*   pattern envelopes for appropriate yardage.)*
Perky Bond Plus interfacing
Do-Sew for stay
Buttons for jacket
Perky Bond, 1 inch wide
Stretch and Sew elastic, 3/4 inch wide for
*   skirts*
Sewing aids listed in Chapter One

Ladies' Suit Jacket

The Ladies' Set-In Sleeve Jacket is a beautiful addition to any wardrobe. The pattern features a cut-on facing and a front button closing. Two collars are included with the pattern: a small rolled collar and a larger rolled collar. The rolled design of the collar makes it fit snugly at the back of the neck.

This jacket is also lovely as a full length coat. Since the pattern already has the correct amount of ease in the hip area, all you need to do to alter the pattern is add the correct amount of length, plus hem, to the front and back pattern pieces.

Determining Your Pattern Size

As with all Stretch & Sew patterns, sizing is by body measurement. If your full bust measurement is 34 inches, then you will select a size 34 pattern. The jacket is made to wear <u>over</u> another garment such as a basic dress, a shell, or a blouse.

I always check the garment length to be sure the pattern is drawn to the preferred length. Necessary alterations are easily made before the pattern is traced. I also suggest that you check the location of the dart on the pattern, making certain that it fits your figure. Adjustments are easily made. Follow the directions for adjustments in Chapter Three, Ladies' Shell, Pattern 350. Trace the pattern pieces on Perky Pattern Paper or Do-Sew pattern material, making any adjustments before cutting. Transfer any pattern markings to the pattern paper.

Cutting Out Your Garment

Place the pattern on the fabric with the greater amount of stretch going across the pattern (around the body). Cut one back, two fronts with cut-on facing, two sleeves, and one collar. Transfer the fold line, dart, and construction marking from the pattern to the garment pieces.

Bound Buttonholes

The strip method for making bound buttonholes is so simple that all the old dreads and fears about making bound buttonholes are gone. Now I know my buttonholes are going to be beautiful. They will be an asset to any garment. If you wish to put bound buttonholes in this garment, they should be made before any sewing is done.

STAY FABRIC

Do-Sew pattern material is a wonderful stay fabric. I recommend that you use it for your bound buttonhole stay. A lightweight woven or non-woven fabric is also satisfactory. This stay should be cut the length of the space where the buttonholes are going to be placed. The strip should measure 2 to 3 inches wider than the finished buttonhole width.

POSITIONING BUTTONS

The position of the buttons on the jacket is determined by your body measurements. One button should be placed at or near the stress point at the high point of the bust. This will eliminate a gap or pulling in this area.

The size of the buttons you choose will determine the number of buttons and buttonholes you will use. Smaller buttons are spaced closer together than large ones. This jacket is not designed to carry a button larger than 1 inch in diameter.

POSITIONING BUTTONHOLES

For a ladies' garment, the buttonholes are always on the right front of the garment. The edge of a horizontal buttonhole should always be 1/8 inch beyond the center front line of the garment with the rest of the buttonhole extending toward the underarm seam. (Fig. 1)

If you carefully position your buttonholes in this manner, the buttons will always line up vertically under your chin in a nice straight line.

The sewn part of the button always moves to the inside of the buttonhole. The distance between the bottom buttonhole and the hem should not be less than the distance between the buttons.

Mark with a pin the position of the buttonholes on the garment. Transfer this marking on the stay fabric after drawing the outlines described below.

THE BUTTONHOLE LADDER

On your stay fabric, draw a line the length of the stay fabric, approximately 5/8 inch from the cut edge. Decide how wide to make your buttonholes and draw a second line that distance away from the first line. When drawing these lines, use a ruler and measure so that both lines are parallel. These two lines are your ladder uprights.

Place this stay fabric on the wrong side of your garment front. Determine exactly where the buttonholes will be positioned, according to the pin marks that you made when previously measuring. At each buttonhole position, draw a horizontal line connecting the two vertical lines drawn on your stay fabric. These horizontal lines are your ladder rungs. (Fig. 2)

Baste-stitch with your sewing machine (or by hand) through the stay fabric and the jacket front, following the lines on your buttonhole ladder. This will transfer the lines through to the right side of your jacket. The threads are easily removed after you sew your buttonholes.

BUTTONHOLE STRIPS

Each buttonhole requires a strip of fabric twice the length of the buttonhole plus 2 inches. For example, a 1-inch buttonhole requires a 4-inch strip. Multiply this strip length by the number of buttonholes. This determines the strip length needed for all of the buttonholes on the garment. The strip should measure 1 inch wide.

1/4-Inch Strip: When you are using bulky fabric or large buttons, you will probably prefer a finished buttonhole strip 1/4 inch wide. Fold the pre-determined length strip in half the long way, wrong sides together. A 1/2 inch wide strip of Perky Bond inserted into the fold and bonded will enable you to sew the strip more accurately.

Sew the folded strip together halfway between the folded line and the cut edge, which is 1/4 inch. Be sure this stitching line is straight. (Fig. 3)

1/8-Inch Strip: When you have chosen a light to medium weight fabric, you will probably prefer a finished buttonhole strip 1/8 inch wide. Fold the pre-determined length strip in half the long way, wrong sides together. A 1/2 inch wide strip of Perky Bond inserted into the fold and bonded will enable you to sew the strip more accurately.

Sew the folded strip together halfway between the folded line and cut edge, which is 1/4 inch. Be sure this stitching is straight. (Fig. 4) Then, sew a second row of stitching halfway between this stitching and the folded edge of the strip. Cut on the first stitching line, leaving a strip 1/4 inch wide. (Fig. 4)

APPLYING THE BOUND BUTTONHOLE

After you have made the strip the desired size, cut the strip into pieces. Each piece should be the size of the buttonhole plus an additional 1 inch. This extra inch gives you a 1/2-inch tab at each end of the buttonhole. (Fig. 5)

Place the garment on a flat surface with the right side of the garment up. The basting stitches,

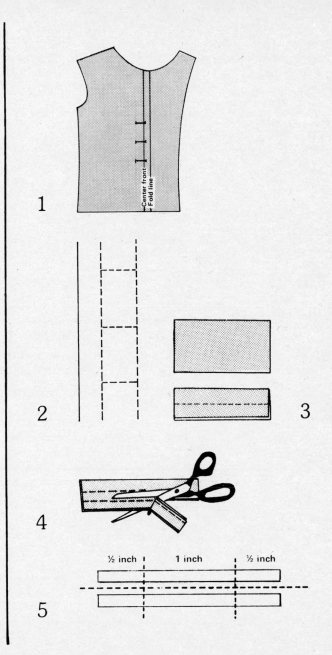

which we refer to as the "buttonhole ladder," will show through so you will know exactly where to position your buttonhole strips.

Position the buttonhole strip on the buttonhole ladder rung, placing the raw edges of the strip along the basting line of the buttonhole ladder. The fold of the buttonhole strip will be out toward the garment and away from the center of the buttonhole.

Stitch this strip to the garment, sewing over the previous stitching line on the buttonhole strip. Backstitch at each edge. Turn the garment over and check to be sure that the stitches are exactly to the edges of the buttonhole ladder and that the line of stitching is straight. (Fig. 6) Straight lines produce straight buttonholes. If you have stitched a little short of the desired length from the wrong side, sew a few more stitches to complete the stitching line. This can be done very easily from the wrong side of the garment.

When you have this strip positioned to your satisfaction, sew the second strip to the buttonhole. This strip is positioned like the first strip. The raw edge is placed on the basting line with the raw edges of both strips touching.

Stitch this strip to the garment, sewing on the stitching line which runs down the center of the buttonhole strips. Turn the garment over again and check the wrong side to be sure the stitching line is the correct length and that it is straight. If it is not correct, fix it now. (Fig. 7)

Continue in this manner until all strips have been sewn to each marked buttonhole on the garment.

After all strips have been sewn to the jacket, cut down the middle of each buttonhole. The cut

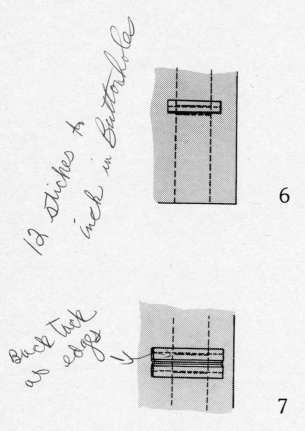

6

7

[handwritten: 12 stiches to inch in Buttonholes]

[handwritten: Back tack at edges]

will go through the front of the garment and through the stay. Begin cutting about 1/4 inch from the other end. Then, cut out to the corners of the stitching line, creating a wedge-shaped piece at each end of each buttonhole. You will need sharp pointed scissors for the cutting. Take care to cut right to the stitching, but not through the stitching. (Fig. 8)

Turn all the strips through the buttonholes to the wrong side of the garment. Gently pull on the ends of the strips to position them evenly. Hand-baste or machine-zigzag the lips of the buttonhole together until the garment is completed to prevent pulling of the buttonholes. (Fig. 9)

Fold the right side of the garment back, exposing the wedge and the strips of fabric at the end of the buttonhole. Stitch through the wedge and the end of the buttonhole strips. (Fig. 10) Avoid sewing through the garment. Repeat this stitching across the wedge and the buttonhole strip of each end of each buttonhole.

After stitching is completed on all the wedges for all the buttonholes, remove the basting stitches and cut away the excess stay fabric around each buttonhole. Trim the tabs of the buttonhole strips to 1/4 inch. Do not finish the backs of the bound buttonholes at this time.

Construction of Your Garment

INTERFACING

Interfacing may be bonded to your garment at this time. The most frequently used procedure for bonding an interfacing is to bond to the facings only. (Fig. 11) To give an entire garment added body, it is possible to bond the entire section to achieve a more tailored effect. (Fig. 12)

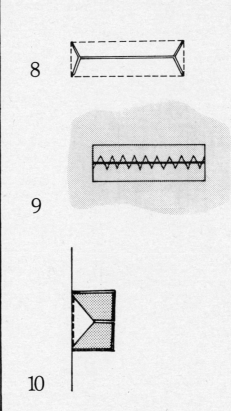

8

9

10

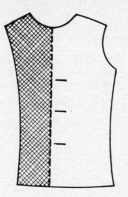

11

12

If you wish to use a Perky Bond Plus interfacing, it should be applied at this time, before seams are sewn. Perky Bond Plus is applied to the wrong side of the undercollar (and to the wrong side of the uppercollar as well for a crisper look) and to the wrong side of the jacket front facing. For the narrow collar, referred to as "Collar A" in the pattern, the Perky Bond Plus should be cut half the depth of the collar pattern and applied to only one-half the depth of the collar. For the wider collar, referred to as "Collar B" in the pattern, Perky Bond Plus is cut to fit the collar pattern.

The front facing is an extension on the jacket front. The Perky Bond Plus should be cut to fit just the facing portion of the pattern, ending at the fold line. Apply Perky Bond Plus to the wrong side of the fabric. (See "Perky Bond Plus Interfacing" directions in Basic Principles.)

DARTS

Sew the darts in the jacket fronts, using a straight stitch. Taper at the end of the darts and chain off at the end. Press the darts toward the bottom of the garment. If you wish to have darts in the back of the jacket, there is an optional dart drawn on the pattern for your convenience. It should be sewn at this time.

SHOULDER SEAMS

Join the shoulder seams. The back seam will be longer than the front to allow for fullness over the shoulder. So, stretch the front seam to meet the back seam. Press the seam open.

COLLAR

If you are making the narrow collar, you should fold the collar in half, right sides together. Sew the end seams, using seam allowances as drawn on the pattern. Trim the under seam allowances to 1/4 inch for a smoother look. Then, clip diagonally across the corners. (Fig. 13)

If you are making the wider collar, place the collar pieces right sides together and pin them in place. Sew around three sides of the collar, making sure the neck edge is left open. Trim the undercollar seam allowance to 1/4 inch and clip diagonally across the corners. (Fig. 14)

Turn the collar right side out and press carefully. Roll the top collar slightly to the underside and press so the seam will not show in the completed garment.

Divide the collar and the jacket back in half and mark with pins. On the outside of the garment, match the center back of the collar to the center back of the jacket and pin them in place, with the undercollar against the right side of the garment. Pin the collar ends at the center front neck edge. Check to be sure the collar ends are at the center front and not at the fold line of the jacket front. Position the collar ends vertically along the center front line of the jacket and pin them in place. Doing this will insure an even collar with collar points that remain properly positioned after the garment is completed.

Baste the collar to the neck edge, beginning at both front edges and basting to the center back.

Fold the facing out over the collar on the fold line, the right side of the facing toward the right side of the garment. Stitch through all thicknesses of the garment, facing, and collar, stitching from the fold line at each front edge to the center back. Overlap the stitches slightly where they meet at the center back. (Fig. 15)

While the facing is in this position, pin it in place at the bottom of the garment. Stitch on the

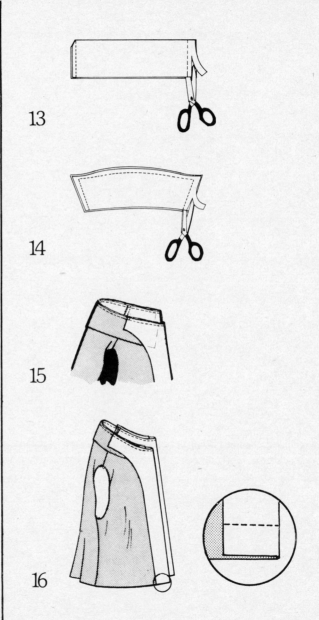

13

14

15

16

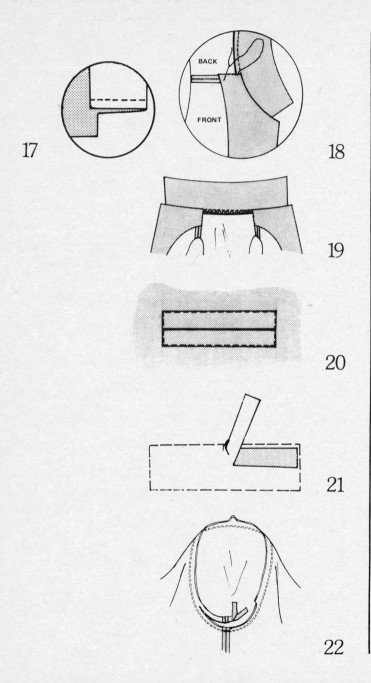

hem allowance line (2 inches from the bottom of the garment), sewing across the bottom facing. Begin stitching at the folded edge and sew to the cut edge. (Fig. 16) Trim close to the stitching. For a smoother look when the garment is finished, grade the facing seam allowance shorter than the garment seam allowance. (Fig. 17)

Turn the facings to the wrong side of the garment and hand tack them to the shoulder seams. Or, bond them in place, using Perky Bond. (Fig. 18)

Trim the underneath seam at the neck edge, leaving the top seam full width. Machine stitch the collar seam allowance between the shoulder seams, sewing 3/8 inch below the previous seam. This stitching, which goes through to the right side of the garment, will be covered by the collar when it is folded down in its finished position. A multiple zigzag stitch is excellent to use in this area. (Fig. 19) Press the facing and the collar carefully.

FINISHING THE BOUND BUTTONHOLES

To finish the buttonholes quickly and easily, pin carefully around all the buttonholes, with the facing in its proper and final position.

On the right side of the garment, "stitch in the ditch" on the inside edge of each buttonhole where the buttonhole strips were sewn to the garment. Sew around the entire square of the buttonhole, lapping stitches slightly at the beginning and end of stitching so this stitching line will not pull out. (Fig. 20)

Working from the wrong side of the garment, cut away the fabric inside the buttonhole, which is inside the "stitch in the ditch" line. Cut right to the stitching line, but do not cut the stitches. (Fig. 21)

Don't worry about the raw edge of the buttonhole where you cut. Knits don't ravel and you won't have any trouble. I have tossed suits in the washer and dryer many times, and the buttonholes are still in perfect condition.

SIDE SEAMS

Place the right side of the garment front to the right side of the garment back with the side seams matching. Pin at the top and the bottom. Sew the side seams, using a straight stitch. These seams should be sewn from the bottom up to the armscye, stretching as you sew. Press the seams open.

SLEEVES

Pin the underarm sleeve at the top and bottom. Match the notches. You will notice that one sleeve seam is longer than the other, with the extra fabric between the notches. This extra fabric is to allow freedom of movement at the elbow. Sew the sleeve seam, stitching from the bottom up to the armscye. Stretch the sleeve seam so that the extra fullness at the elbow area is smooth and unwrinkled. Since this is a stress seam, you must be sure to stretch the seam as you sew it.

Press the seam open. Be sure the sleeve seam and underarm seam of the jacket are thoroughly pressed and remain in an open position when removed from the ironing board. A sleeve board will be of help to you when pressing the sleeve seam open.

Set the sleeve into the armcye with right sides together. Match the notched top of the sleeve to the shoulder seam of the jacket. Pin them into place. Match the underarm seam of the sleeve with the side seam of the jacket. Pin it into place.

In the past, the normal process has been to sew with the garment positioned properly on the top and the sleeve on the bottom. But since the armscye is closed, it is difficult to do this. I have found it quite simple to sew this sleeve in by stretching the under portion and sewing with the sleeve on top. When using a firmer fabric with restricted stretch, sew a row of gathering stitches across the cap of the sleeve. This will help to ease the sleeve into the armscye more evenly. Stretch the seam as you sew. Try on the garment to be sure the shoulder seam is positioned properly for your figure.

Sew a second row of stitching 1/8 inch from the previous line of stitching, inside the seam allowance. Stretch this second seam as it is sewn. Then, trim the entire armscye seam allowance to 1/4 inch. Lightly press the seam toward the sleeve. (Fig. 22)

HEM

Press the hem into place. Pressing is vitally important here. The jacket will not have a well-tailored look unless it is properly pressed. The hem may be sewn with a handcatch stitch or by bonding in place.

MACHINE-STITCHED BUTTONHOLES

If you are going to make machine-stitched buttonholes, they should be sewn now. Remember that one buttonhole should be positioned over the high point of the bust with the others spaced evenly. Be sure you put the buttonholes on the right front of the garment.

Sew the buttons on the left side of the jacket front, on the center front line. Press the jacket carefully.

SEPARATE FACING

The cut-on facing featured in this pattern eliminates a seam and bulk at the front edge of the jacket. If you wish, a separate facing can be cut and sewn on. This technique is often used for a separate color for the lapel. You will need to add seam allowances to both the jacket front and the facing at the fold line. To maintain a professional appearance, topstitch the garment along the front edge seam.

Ladies' Gored Skirts

Pattern 425 contains three different skirts. One is a multi-gored skirt which features many small gores and gives the appearance of a pleated skirt. The four-gored skirts are a graceful A-line and the A-line flip skirt.

Multi-Gored Skirt

I have seen this pattern made in a variety of sizes, from 3 year olds to ladies with a 33-inch waist, and, of course, the sizes in between. All looked lovely. This skirt is comfortable to wear and very smart looking. The multi-gored skirt design makes up nicely in wool and wool and polyester blends and acrylics.

The uniqueness of this skirt design is seen in the gores which taper from 2-1/2 inches at the waist to 4-1/2 inches at the hem. This design provides an almost straight skirt, with walking ease at the knee.

Determining Your Pattern Size

This pattern has only one piece, and the piece is the same for all sizes. Each gore measures 2-1/2 inches at the waist and 4-1/2 inches at the hem. The finished gore after stitching will measure 2x4 inches. To determine how to cut your skirt, measure your waist, and add 4 to 6 inches to this measurement. For example, if your waist measurement is 24 inches, add 4 to 6 inches.

(Four inches is adequate for a soft, stretchy fabric. Six inches is better for a firmer knit or for a freer hanging skirt.) Dividing the total number (28 to 30) in half will give you the correct number of gores needed. Fourteen gores for a soft, stretchy knit; 15 for a firmer knit.

Check the skirt length. It is very difficult to adjust this hem after the skirt is completed. When measuring, remember that the pattern allows 1-1/2 inches at the top for elastic and 2 inches at the bottom for the hem. Any length adjustment must be made at the "shorten or lengthen" line indicated on the pattern. Do not adjust at the hem.

Cut the required number of gores. The center line of each gore must be on the straight of the fabric.

Construction of Your Garment

Fold each gore in half, lengthwise, wrong sides together. Press each gore down the center. Press very carefully with a damp cloth to insure a good crease. (Fig. 23)

After all the gores are pressed, sew the gores together. Right sides together, stitch from the wide end at the bottom to the narrow end at the top, stretching as you sew. Carefully maintain the proper seam width throughout your sewing. (Fig. 24)

After all the gores are joined together, clip each seam allowance 4 inches from the bottom edge of each gore (for the hem) and 1-1/2 inches from the top edge on each gore (for elastic). Press the bottom 4-inch seam allowance open from the bottom of the gore up to the clipped area. (Fig. 25)

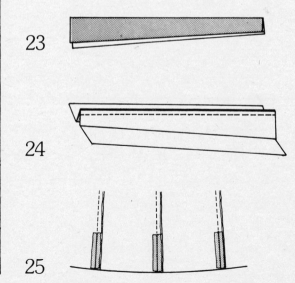

23

24

25

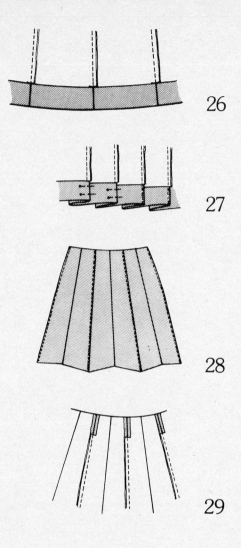

26

27

28

29

HEM

Fold up and press the 2-inch hem allowance in place. The pressed-open seam area at the bottom of the gores will now be covered with the hem. (Fig. 26) Fold the gores right sides together at the seam lines and stitch each gore from the bottom fold of the hem to the top of the hem. Join this stitching to the previous stitching. (Fig. 27)

On the right side of the garment, stitch along the pressed-in crease of each gore, using either a single or a double needle. (Stitching with a single needle on a crease will give you a sharper pleat.) Sew from the bottom of each gore up through the double thickness of the hem to the waist edge. On this one seam, you must leave the fabric in its relaxed position. Do not stretch this seam. No other hemming is necessary on this skirt. The stitching at the seam line and the crease hold the skirt hem in place beautifully. (Fig. 28) The multi-gored skirt is also soft and lovely without topstitching.

WAIST ELASTIC

Press the top 1-1/2-inch seam allowance open from the top of each gore down to the clipped area. (Fig. 29)

Cut Stretch and Sew 3/4-inch waist elastic 1 inch shorter than the body waist measurement. Lap the ends of the waist elastic 1/2 inch and stitch securely. Divide the elastic and skirt top in fourths and mark with pins or pencil dots. Match the divisions and pin the elastic in place, even with the inside top edge of the skirt.

Using a zigzag stitch (or using a straight stitch and stretching hard as you sew), sew the elastic to the skirt, stitching around the entire upper edge. Stretch both thicknesses as you sew. Fold the elastic over to the inside of the skirt. Be careful to keep the elastic and the fold line even. Stitch again, over the first line of stitching, through all thicknesses. (Fig. 30)

Four-Gored Skirts

The patterns for the four-gored skirts included in Pattern 425 are designed to make a well-fitted skirt with comfortable walking ease. Choose a fabric with good stretch so that it will pull on and off easily.

Determining Your Pattern Size

This skirt pattern is designed by hip size. Measure from your waist down 9 inches. Measure around the hip. If you measure 38 inches, you should choose the size 38 pattern.

Pre-determine the finished length for your skirt before tracing the pattern. There is a dotted line at the hip area marked "shorten or lengthen." Any length adjustment should be made at this line. Remember to allow 1-1/2 inches for the elastic waistband plus the hem allowance when checking the skirt length.

Cut 4 gores with the stretch going across the pattern (around the body).

Construction of Your Garment

Sew the gores, right sides together, from the bottom up to the top, stretching the seam as you sew. Press open the seam allowance.

If you have worn skirts which form a fold of fabric across the small of the back (Fig. 31), a good way to eliminate this is to cut the back of the skirt down at the waistline. Begin cutting at the center back, 1/2 to 1 inch from the top of the skirt, tapering gradually up to the sides. (Fig. 32)

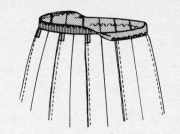

30

31

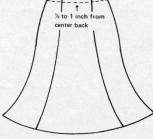

32

Elastic is sewn to the four-gored skirt in the same manner as it is sewn to the multi-gored skirt. Refer to the multi-gored skirt section in this chapter for directions.

TO HEM THE FOUR-GORED SKIRT

If you have made the four-gored skirt in the A-line, the hem is pressed in place and sewn with a handcatch stitch or bonded, using Perky Bond and following the bonding instructions in Basic Principles.

TO HEM THE FOUR-GORED FLIP SKIRT

If you have made the flip skirt, a different technique is used for hemming. A small hem is allowed to avoid extra bulk when turning. Using stretch lace, sew the lace to the right side of the lower skirt edge, stretching the lace as it is sewn. By allowing the skirt to remain in a relaxed position and stretching the lace, the fullness at the hemline will be eased in. (Fig. 33) When the hem is pinned in position, it will lie flat and smooth. Again, pressing is imperative. Allow the steam to do the work and press this hem carefully. Bond the hem in place with Perky Bond or stitch by hand using a catch stitch.

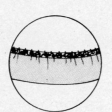

33

8

Ladies' One-Piece Swim Suit
Ladies' Two-Piece Swim Suit

Introduction

For many years, swim suits have been an important part of our Stretch and Sew lessons. My first experience with a swim suit was with one I made for our daughter Kris when she was a young teenager on her way to Arizona with her dad. The swim suit really looked great as Kris was packing it into her bag for the trip. When the water test came, we learned one important lesson. Rayon elastic will not hold its size when wet! Kris made a great dive but her exit from the pool left something to be desired.

A few years later, I discovered some elastic made for swim wear, and again I tried my luck with a suit. This time I made one for myself. I chose a wool double knit. The natural stretch of this fabric seemed to be perfect for a swim suit. The water test that I gave the suit in my shower before I made a public appearance with it worked great and I thought I had the answer. Well, wool double knit dries very slowly and all too often I found myself trying to get into a wet suit.

Those were all important experiences for me when I was learning to sew knit fabrics. With the vast knowledge we have today, I often marvel at the nerve I must have had to try the things I did. As we begin the final lesson in our Basic 8 series, let me say that I am truly happy you have chosen the Stretch and Sew way to sew. I certainly hope the things that you have learned — and will learn in the future — will bring you as much pleasure as they have brought me.

Ladies' One-Piece Swim Suit
Ladies' Two-Piece Swim Suit

For your eighth Stretch and Sew class you will need:

Ladies' One-Piece Swim Suit, Pattern 1300
Ladies' Two-Piece Swim Suit, Pattern 1350
Perky Pattern Paper or Do-Sew
Swim fabric (See fabric discussion in this chapter)
Swim lining (See lining discussion in this chapter)
Stretch and Sew elastic
Bra cups
Swim hook (for two-piece suit)
Fold-over trim (optional)
Sewing aids listed in Chapter One

Selection of Fabric

Because of the quick drying characteristics of nylon double knit plus the great elasticity of the fabric, we often select this fabric for many of our specially designed Stretch and Sew swim prints.

Most nylon double knits will easily stretch to at least half again their original size. For example, 10 inches of fabric will stretch to 15 – 17 inches. With firmer fabrics there is less tendency to stretch and a larger size pattern is needed. The opposite is true when a very stretchy fabric is used. If the fabric you choose is extremely stretchy, stretching to double its size (10 inches stretching to 20 inches), it is wise to use a smaller size pattern.

At first, this may seem a bit confusing, so let your Stretch and Sew Fabric Center sales people help you. Then, after you have made a few suits, you will be making the decisions yourself.

A special swim lining is manufactured for the Stretch and Sew Fabric Centers that has excellent drying characteristics as well as good two-way stretch. It is best to use this lining in your suit since a lining with just one-way stretch could cause some problems.

Stretch and Sew swim suit patterns include approximately 4 inches of stretch over the hip area in each size. For example, a size 12 suit is designed to fit a woman with a 36 inch hip. But the suit, after seams are sewn, measures 32 inches at the hips. As a result, the suit will stay smooth-fitting when it's wet. Wet fabrics have a tendency to relax and the stretch designed into the pattern helps retain a smooth fit. Maximum stretch must always go around the body. For the one-piece suit, a two-way stretch fabric is a must. The two-piece suit will fit well when made of a fabric with either a one-way or a two-way stretch.

Ladies' One-Piece Swim Suit with Skirt and Lining

Determining Your Pattern Size

The proper length of the one-piece suit is vitally important if a good overall fit is to be achieved. The following steps will help you achieve this vertical fit:

check mat. for stretch over body. — For second skin material subtract 6" for regular swim material subtract 4"

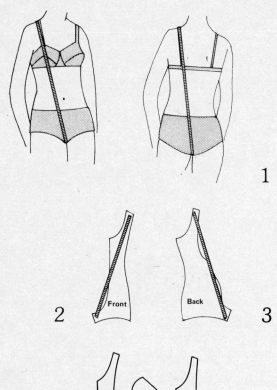

1

2 Front   Back 3

4

1. Measure the body from the center of the right shoulder, through the crotch, to the center of the left shoulder. (Fig. 1) This should be a comfortable measurement — not too loose or too tight.

2. Depending on the vertical stretch of the fabric, subtract 2 to 6 inches from this total measurement. (A one-piece suit should stretch up on to the shoulders.)

3. Measure the front on your correct pattern size from the shoulder strap (minus the seam allowance) down to the center of the crotch (minus the seam allowance). (Fig. 2)

4. Hold the tape measure at that spot and move to the back pattern piece of the correct size. Continue the measurement from the crotch back (minus the seam allowance) to the center of the shoulder strap (minus the seam allowance). (Fig. 3)

5. If this pattern measurement is the same as your body measurement, you are ready to continue.

6. If you need to shorten or lengthen your pattern, do the following:
   a. Divide your front, side panel, and back pattern pieces in equal thirds. (Fig. 4)
   b. This gives you six breaks in your pattern pieces.
   c. Divide into <u>four</u> equal parts the amount of difference between the body measurement and the pattern measurement. Add or subtract to the pattern at the division line. For example, if the body measurement is 58 inches and the pattern measurement is 56 inches, you would add 1/2 inch to each pattern division point for the correct distribution of length.

Trace your correct size on Perky Pattern Paper or Do-Sew pattern material. You will need a skirt front panel, side front panel, back section, and front section cut only up to the dotted line at the waist. Transfer any pattern markings.

Cutting Swim Fabric

Some nylon double knits are finished in a tube with a permanent crease. If your fabric is still in tube form, be careful not to use the permanent crease as a center front. Slit the tube of fabric along one of the permanent crease lines and refold to cut the skirt front section.

Place the pattern on the double thickness of fabric with the greater stretch going around the body. Cut one skirt along the fold line, two side front sections, two back sections, and two front sections (waist high). A dotted line on the pattern indicates the cutting line for the center front section. Transfer the markings to your fabric. (Fig. 5)

If you wish to match a pattern (a stripe, for instance), it will be necessary to cut each piece separately. Be certain that you reverse each piece for the opposite side when you are only cutting one piece at a time.

Cutting Lining Fabric

If your swim suit fabric is sheer and you wish to line the entire suit, you should cut the lining for the skirt front (even with the bottom of the straps), lining for the side fronts (up to the bottom of the bust area), lining for the back sections (up to the bottom of the straps), and lining for the center front section. Usually, only the crotch area is lined in the suit center front section. This is the technique we will learn.

To line the crotch area, it will be necessary to

5

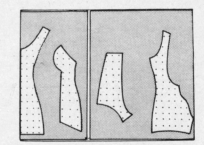

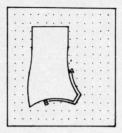

6

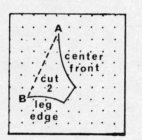

7

make a pattern from the swim suit front section. Place your swim suit front pattern on a piece of dotted paper and draw along the center front line from the bottom up to a point halfway to the waist edge (a) and to a point halfway on the leg edge (b). (Fig. 6)

Remove your pattern and join the line at the top (a) with the point where you stopped at the leg edge (b). Use a straight edge to join these points. From this pattern, cut two crotch lining pieces with the stretch going crosswise. (Fig. 7)

Seams and Stitches

All swim suit seams are stress seams. It is important to be sure that all of the seams will stretch. If you are sewing the seam with a straight stitch machine, be certain you have stretched the seam as far as you will be stretching it in wearing. A second line of stitching 1/8 inch from the first is recommended for reinforcement. Stretch this second stitching also.

It is possible to sew a suit with a fine zigzag stitch. When this stitch is used, you will not stretch the seam as you sew since the thread build-up would cause the seam to ruffle. A straight stretch stitch is an excellent stitch for a swim suit, but it should be used only when a good fit is assured. This seam is difficult to remove. When a straight stretch stitch is used, it is necessary to sew the seam only one time and it is unnecessary to stretch the fabric. This special stitch is available on our Stretch & Sew sewing machine.

Thread

Use a synthetic thread when sewing swim wear. The strength of the synthetic fibers will give you longer wear.

Construction of Your Garment

THE FRONT SECTION AND SKIRT

With the right sides together, sew the center front seam of the front section from the crotch to the waist. (Fig. 8)

Place the center front section, right sides together, on a flat surface. On top of the front sections, place <u>both</u> lining pieces, right sides together, with the cut edges of the seam allowances even. Pin them into place. Turn the garment over and sew again over the previous stitching line, sewing through all thicknesses. (Fig. 9)

Fold the lining over the seam into position, matching the cut edges of the lining to the cut edges of the leg area. This technique produces a neatly enclosed seam. Pin the lining to the wrong side of the front section and treat the two pieces of fabric as one. (Fig. 10)

Position the lining to the wrong side of the skirt panel and treat the skirt panel as one piece. To keep your skirt hem smooth, use a piece of 3/8-inch swim suit elastic at the hem of the skirt panel. Cut the elastic the width of the skirt panel at the hemline. Place it on the wrong side of the skirt panel and sew it into place, stitching along the bottom edge of elastic and skirt panel. (Fig. 11) Turn the elastic over and sew again along the previous stitching line.

Place the center front sections, right side up, on a flat surface. Over this, place the skirt panel, right side up, with the hem of the skirt panel positioned 3/8 inch above the cut edge of the center front leg sections. (When the legs are hemmed with 3/8-inch elastic, the front and skirt sections will be exactly the same length.) Pin the two sections together and treat them as one unit. (Fig. 12)

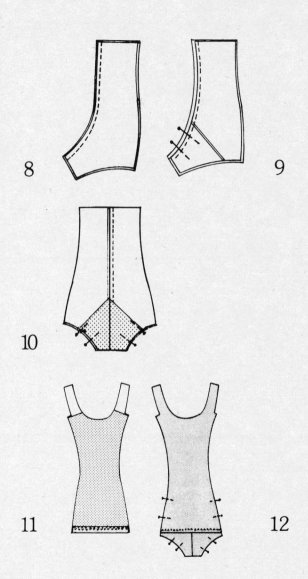

8   9

10

11   12

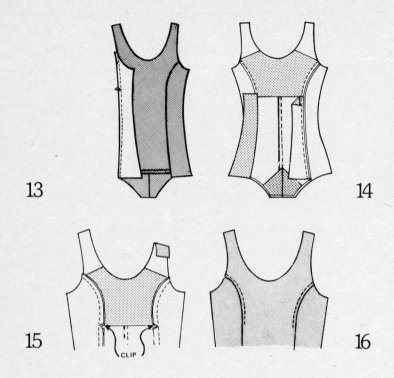

13

14

15   CLIP

16

SIDE FRONT PANEL

Pin the side front panels to the center front panel, right sides together, matching the notches. Stitch through all thicknesses. (Fig. 13)

The side front lining has been cut even with the notch in the seam. Place the side front lining on top of the front lining, the cut edges even. Sew along the previous stitching lines. When the side front lining is folded back into position, this seam is also enclosed. (Fig. 14)

Clip the seam at a point below the bust and fold the seam allowance above the clip toward the center of the suit. (Fig. 15)

From the right side, topstitch 1/8 inch from the seam, beginning at the point where you clipped and stitching to the armscye. (Fig. 16)

BATHING SUIT BRA CUP

We have found a bra cup that we feel is the finest available for swim wear. This bra cup is made of a molded polyester fiber and is extremely durable. You should choose a bra cup to correspond with the size of the suit — with one exception. If you have used a smaller size pattern to accommodate a very stretchy fabric, the cup size should remain the same as the suit size would be if a fabric with normal stretch were used. The same is true if the suit size was increased to accommodate a fabric with little stretch. Again, the cup size remains constant and only the pattern size is changed.

In response to many requests, Stretch and Sew Fabric Centers now carry mastectomy bust pads that are especially manufactured for use in swim suits. Made of polyester, these surgical bust pads are lightweight and very comfortable and have been a boon to women who wish to make their own suits but needed the additional pad. A smooth, triacetate jersey cover supplied with each bust pad is so carefully made that no seams touch the body. The unique design of this cover creates a wrinkle-free bust pad that provides assurance and comfort to the wearer. The dacron filler dries rapidly.

The front of the bathing suit has now been sewn together. The bra cups <u>must</u> be positioned at this time, before the next seams are sewn.

Enclosed with the bra cup kit is a pattern. Place the pattern on a flat surface. Position the power net over the pattern. (The pattern will be visible through the power net.) The edge of the power net should be at the bottom edge of the pattern. Place the bra cups in position with the softer side next to the power net. (Fig. 17) Zigzag or straight stitch the bra cups to the power net. Trim away the power net which covers the inside of the bra cups. (Fig. 18)

On the one-piece suit, Pattern 1300, the bottom edge of the bra cup is not sewn into a seam, so we will add some soft felt-backed elastic to this edge. Felt-backed elastic is available in several widths. I prefer using the 1-inch elastic in my suits. A lady with a heavy bust might be more comfortable using the 2-inch elastic. Measure the lingerie elastic the same length as the power net under the bra cups. A piece of elastic this length will hold your bra cups in the proper position when sewn into the side seams.

Place the felt side of the elastic to the inside of the garment, along the bottom of the power net, with the elastic lapped 1/4 inch over the power net. Stitch along the top edge of the elastic, using a zigzag stitch. Do not stretch as you sew. If you must sew with a straight stitch, stretch both fabric and elastic equally. (Fig. 19)

17
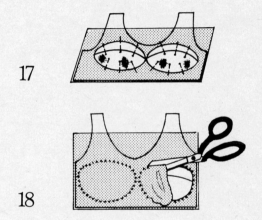

18

19
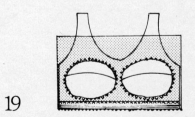

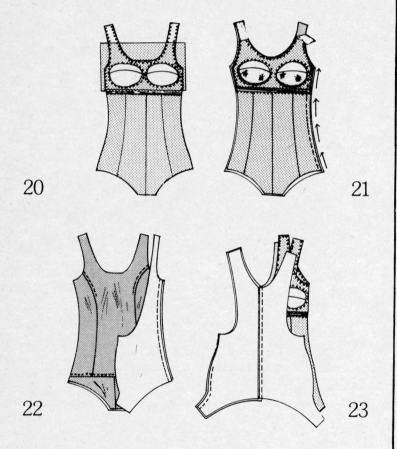

20

21

22

23

After sewing the elastic to the bottom of the power net, position the power net on the wrong side of the swim suit. Be sure the swim suit fabric is pinned smoothly over the bra cups before you begin stitching. Stitch along the armscye and the front neck edge, sewing along the cut edge of the suit with a fine zigzag stitch. (Fig. 20)

Trim around the top of the swim suit, cutting away the power net, being careful not to cut the zigzag stitching.

SIDE SEAMS AND BACK SECTION

Pin the front to the back at the side seams, right sides together. The front lining is to be included with this seam, as well as the power net and felt-backed elastic from the bra cup area. Sew all the layers together, stitching from the bottom up to the armscye. (Fig. 21)

Position the back lining on top of the seam over the front section of the suit. Sew over the previous stitching, through the swim fabric, lining and power net. When this seam is sewn, the side seam will be enclosed. (Fig. 22)

Sew the center back seam of the swim suit from the crotch area up approximately half way. The lining is not included in this seam at this time. Baste the crotch seam and try on the suit to check the strap length. (Fig. 23)

After the correct strap length has been determined, sew the shoulder seams. (Fig. 24) Finger press the seam open. Finish sewing the center back seam.

Remove the basting stitches at the crotch area and turn the suit inside out. Place one back lining piece on the center back seam with the cut edge of the lining even with the cut edge of the center back of the suit. Now bring the other piece of back lining around the entire suit, so that it is on top of the first piece of lining. You should have four layers of fabric: 2 layers of swim suit fabric and then 2 layers of lining fabric. Sew over the previous stitching line, through all four thicknesses. (Fig. 25) Turn the suit right side out (through the 2 back lining pieces). When the suit is in the correct position, the center back seam will also be enclosed.

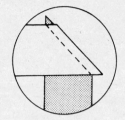

24

Pin the crotch seam with right sides together. Be sure that you pin at both edges and at the center. Stretch the seams to match when sewing and stitch with a 5/8 inch seam allowance. Trim the back seam allowance to 1/4 inch. Press the front seam over the back seam of the suit. Welt stitch 1/2 inch from the original crotch seam, sewing through all thicknesses. Trim to the stitching line.

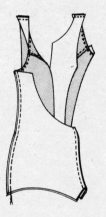

25

APPLYING THE ELASTIC

Stretch and Sew elastic comes in 1/4-inch, 3/8-inch, and 3/4-inch widths and has been treated to withstand chlorine. It is completely washable and dry cleanable and will not lose its stretch when wet.

For women's swim suits, I prefer the 3/8-inch elastic for arm, neck, and leg edges and 3/4-inch elastic for waists.

To apply the elastic to neck and arm areas, sew 3/8-inch wide elastic to the wrong side of the swim suit. With the edge of the elastic even with the cut edge of fabric, sew along the cut edge, using a zigzag stitch, if available. (Fig. 26) The ratio of elastic to the suit is 1:1 except on the curved areas at the back waist and the front neck. The back waist should have 2 inches less elastic

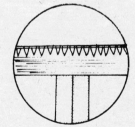

26

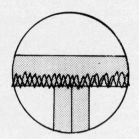

27

28

than the curve measurement. The front neck should have 2 to 3 inches less elastic than the curve measures. Around the armscye, you should use a 1:1 ratio.

Fold the elastic to the inside of the suit, which will cover the elastic with swim suit fabric. Sew along the previous stitching line, using a zigzag stitch, if available. It is vital that your stitches encase the raw edge of the swim fabric and the edge of the elastic. (Fig. 27) If the stitches do not overlap the edge of the elastic, it will have a tendency to roll up. It is also important that the final zigzag stitching includes the bra cup edges along the front neckline and the armscye.

To apply elastic to the leg, sew 3/8-inch elastic to the leg opening, attaching it as above. For the correct length, cut the elastic 1 inch less than the measurement and apply it to the leg opening with a 1:1 ratio at the front and sides. Stretch the elastic at the back of the leg. Place the edge of the elastic even with the cut edge of the fabric. Sew along the cut edge, using a zigzag stitch, if available.

When you apply the elastic to the leg, you should be careful not to catch the skirt panel in your second row of stitching.

It will be necessary to fold the skirt section out of the way to begin this stitching. Start sewing at the seam line on the front panel under the skirt. Sew around the inside leg edge to a point close to the seam line at the skirt section.

Fold the elastic to the inside of the suit. This will cover the elastic with swim suit fabric. Sew along the previous stitching line, using a zigzag stitch, if available. (Fig. 28)

Ladies' One-Piece Suit without Skirt

(FULLY LINED)

If you wish to make a one-piece suit without a skirt, follow the previous directions, omitting all reference to a skirt. Remember to cut 2 complete front sections and do not cut a skirt front. Construction details will be the same.

Ladies' One-Piece Suit with Skirt

(LINED IN THE CROTCH AREA ONLY)

Follow the previous cutting instructions, but do not cut the lining pieces. If you are using an opaque fabric and wish to line only the crotch area, it will be necessary to make a pattern from the swim suit front section. Place your swim suit front pattern on a piece of dotted paper and draw along the center front line from the bottom up to a point halfway to the waist. (Fig. 29a) Following the seam line, trace out halfway along the leg edge. (Fig. 29b) Remove your pattern and join the line at the top (Fig. 29a) with the point where you stopped at the leg edge. (Fig. 29b) Use a straight edge to join these points. (Fig. 30) From this pattern, cut two crotch lining pieces with the stretch going across.

Nylon tricot will be satisfactory when lining only the crotch area, but you should not use it to line the entire suit. Nylon tricot has no vertical stretch and will spoil the appearance and fit of your suit.

Construction of Your Garment

With right sides together, sew the center front seam of the front section, sewing from the crotch up to the top of the center front panel. (Fig. 31)

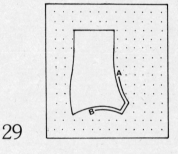

29

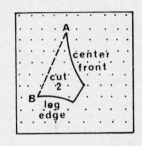

30

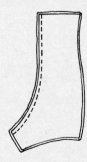

31

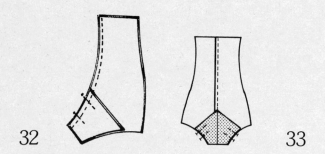

32

33

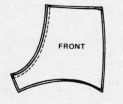

FRONT

34

Place the center front section, right sides together, on a flat surface. Place <u>both</u> crotch lining pieces (right sides together) on top of the front sections with the cut edges of the seam allowances even. Pin them in place. Turn the garment over and sew again over the previous stitching line, sewing through all thicknesses. (Fig. 32)

Fold the lining over the seam into position, matching the cut edges of the lining to the cut edges of the leg area. Pin it in position at the sides of the front panel and include it in the seam when sewing the front panel to the side front. (Fig. 33)

For construction details, follow directions under the "Ladies' Swim Suit with Front Skirt" section, omitting the reference to lining.

Ladies' Two-Piece Swim Suit

A two-piece suit usually has the swim suit bottom lined completely and the bra section lined by the molded bra cups. The following instructions will show you the enclosed seam finish for lining the swim suit bottoms for a very comfortable suit. If you prefer, you may line just the crotch section, making a pattern for this piece following the preceding instructions.

Determining Your Pattern Size

Refer to the section on pattern sizing at the beginning of this chapter. Trace the pattern pieces on Do-Sew pattern material or Perky Pattern Paper, using the correct size pattern.

Construction of Your Garment

SWIM SUIT BOTTOM AND LINING

With the right sides together, sew the center front seam. Sew from the crotch seam up to the waist. (Fig. 34)

Leaving the fronts in this position, place <u>both</u> front linings (right sides together) on top of the pant fronts with the cut edges even. You now have 4 pieces of fabric in this order: 2 pieces of swim fabric, right sides together, and 2 pieces of lining fabric, right sides together. (Fig. 35)

Stitch along the previous seam, sewing through all four thicknesses. (Fig. 36) Open the lining and the swim suit bottoms into position. The center front seam will be enclosed. Sew the swim suit bottom backs in the same manner, including the step for the lining.

To join the front to the back, place the right sides of the swim suit bottoms together. Sew one side seam of the swim suit but <u>do not</u> include the lining in this seam. (Fig. 37)

Pin one edge of the lining into position at the side seam, the cut edges. even. Wrap the other edge of lining completely around the suit, meeting the seam. You will now have 2 pieces of swim fabric together and 2 pieces of lining fabric together with the suit rolled up inside. (Fig. 38) Sew along the previous stitching line, sewing through all 4 thicknesses. One side seam will be enclosed. (Repeat for the other side seam, with the right sides of the swim suit bottoms together.)

For the crotch seam, sew through the swim suit fabric and the lining with a 5/8 inch seam allowance. Press the seam toward the back of the garment. Welt stitch this seam, sewing through all thicknesses as described for the one-piece suit. Trim the excess fabric to the stitching line. (Fig. 39)

APPLYING THE ELASTIC

Measure your waist. Cut Stretch and Sew 3/4-inch elastic three inches shorter than this measurement.

Lap the elastic 1/2 inch, forming a circle, and

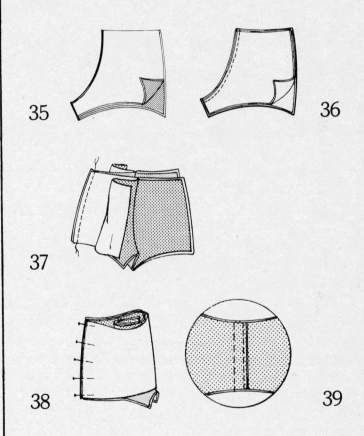

35 36 37 38 39

join it together with machine stitching. Divide the elastic and the waist edges into equal fourths and mark with pins or pencil dots. Match the divisions and pin the elastic to the garment. The top edge of the elastic should be even with the top edge of the garment. Stitch along the top edge, stretching the elastic to fit the garment. Use a zigzag or multiple zigzag stitch. If a zigzag stitch is unavailable, then you will need to stretch both the fabric and the elastic. Turn the elastic to the inside of the garment and stitch again along the same stitching line. Be careful to catch both the elastic and the swim suit in a zigzag stitch. This will produce a neatly covered elastic edge at the waist of the swim suit bottoms.

For the legs of the two-piece suit, use Stretch and Sew 3/8-inch elastic. The leg elastic is sewn with a 1:1 ratio except at the back of the leg. In this area, 2 inches less elastic will insure a snug fit. The elastic is applied using the same technique as previously described.

SWIM SUIT TOP

The first seam to sew on the swim suit top attaches the side panel to the center front section. Sew with a fine zigzag stitch or stretch slightly and sew with a straight stitch. Sew with right sides together. (Fig. 40) Finger press the seam allowance toward the center and topstitch 1/8 inch from the seam. Work on the right side of the garment. Stitch the opposite side panel in the same manner. (Fig. 40)

BRA CUPS

Bra cups are sewn to the power net and attached to the front of the suit using the same techniques as for the one-piece suit. Omit the felt-back elastic application. (Figs. 41 & 42)

Sew the side seams of the top, joining the

front and back, stitching through the power net and the garment seam allowances. (Fig. 43) Fold the seams to the back and welt stitch. (Fig. 44)

The top should be tried on to check the shoulder strap length and the position of the back hook. After the correct strap length has been determined, the shoulder strap is sewn and the seam is pressed open. (Fig. 45)

ELASTIC FOR THE SWIM SUIT TOP

The neck, armscye, and bottom edge of the swim suit top must be finished with 3/8-inch Stretch and Sew elastic, applied in the same manner as the elastic on the suit bottom. The armscye ratio is 1:1. Sew without stretching, using a zigzag stitch. The neckline requires a 1:1 ratio except in the curve of the front neckline. Here, the elastic should be 2 to 3 inches less than the curve. The elastic is stitched with a medium zigzag stitch and then turned to the inside and stitched a second time. (Fig. 46) It is important that the final zigzag stitch includes the cup edge along the front neckline, the armscye, and the bottom edge. (Fig. 47)

Apply the elastic around the bottom edge of the swim suit bodice on a 1:1 ratio.

BRA HOOK

Fold the ends of the back strap 1 inch to the inside of the garment, forming a loop with the left side. Attach the swim suit hook to the right side. Sew it securely with machine stitching. The fabric loop on the left side will slip through the hook to fasten the suit. (Fig. 48)

Fold-Over Swim Trim

I would like to introduce you to our nylon fold-over trim. Nylon fibers are used for this trim

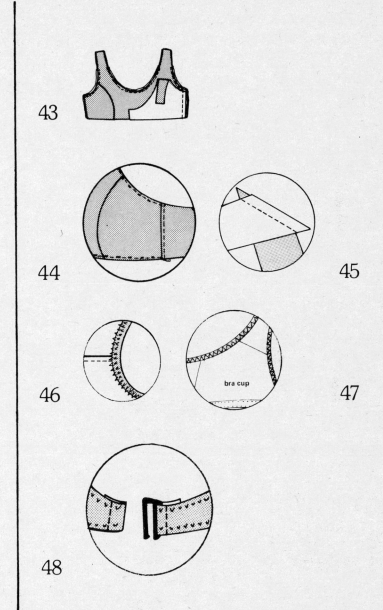

43

44

45

46

47

bra cup

48

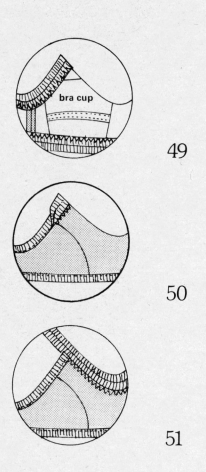

49

50

51

because it is possible to dye nylon in such clear and bright colors. It is available in a wide range of colors and provides a neatly trimmed edge for a swim suit.

This trim does not have the same stretch as elastic and will not serve as a waist finish. Shoulder straps are perfect uses of the trim; armscye and neck edges also add interest to an otherwise plain garment. If you are using a fold-over trim, it is not necessary to put elastic in the area you are trimming.

To apply the fold-over trim, remove the seam allowance where the trim will be applied. Sew the trim to the wrong side of the garment. (Fig. 49) Turn it over and topstitch on the right side. The main trick to putting on this trim is to pay attention to the raw edge. It must not extend beyond the fold in the trim. Carefully trim away any excess seam allowance before folding the trim to the right side for the second stitching. (Fig. 50) If your fold-over trim is not folded exactly in half, use the narrower side underneath, folding the wider side over to the top. Use a multiple zigzag stitch. If that is not available, zigzag is a second choice. If neither is available, you can use a straight stitch. But remember, this area is stretched a great deal when pulled on and off and the sewing will have to give with the garment. So you must stretch the trim and the suit equally for both stitchings. Since trim is rather difficult to splice, I always try to arrange the trim so the ends can be sewn into a seam, eliminating a splice. (Fig. 51)

To create a shoulder strap and add trim to the entire suit top, you must apply the trim in a specific order.

1. Cut off the straps allowed on the pattern.

2. Apply the trim to the underarm area. (Fig. 52)

3. Beginning at the center back of the suit, stitch to where the back shoulder strap would normally originate.

4. Try on the suit to get a shoulder strap length. Pin the trim to the front neck edge where the front shoulder strap would normally originate, to mark the length. Remember to make this strap snug. When wet, the trim holds its shape well but does loosen slightly.

5. Continue sewing the trim across the front neck edge of the suit. Measure the length of the first shoulder strap and allow this amount for the second strap. Continue stitching across the back edge of the suit.

6. The bottom edge of the suit may also be finished with trim. Ease the swim suit into the trim under the bra cup to keep a snug fit. Use 2 inches less trim than swim suit in the front section. (Fig. 53)

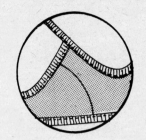

52

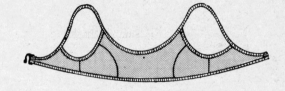

53

Facts on Fibers

Natural Fibers

Generic Name	Use	Characteristics	Care
Alpaca	Sweaters Shawls Dresses Shrinks	Blended with wool. Warm, resilient, and absorbent. Good shape retention and wrinkle recovery.	Dry cleaning recommended. See Chapter 5 for blocking instructions.
Cotton	Knit tops Ladies' and children's outerwear and underwear Rib trim	Soft to the touch. Durable, absorbent, "breathes". Resists moths, heat, and perspiration.	Machine wash 8-10 minutes in warm water. Tumble dry, remove promptly.
Linen	Outerwear including Slacks Skirts Jackets Dresses Men's wear	Most commonly found as a blend with polyester in knit fabrics.	If linen content is minimal, treat fabric according to care instructions for the major fiber of the blend.
Silk	Outerwear including Slacks Skirts Jackets Dresses Men's wear	Wild silk (Tussah): Most commonly found as a blend with polyester in knit fabrics. Usually creates a slubbed or knobby appearance to the fabric.	If silk content is minimal, treat fabric according to care instructions for the major fiber of the blend.
Wool	Outerwear including Slacks Skirts Jackets Dresses Men's wear	Durable and warm with excellent memory. Resists wrinkles, holds sharp crease.	Dry cleaning recommended.

Synthetic Fibers

Generic Name	Use	Characteristics	Care
Acrylic	Outerwear including Slacks Sweaters Coats Suits Dresses Children's wear	Bright colors. Durable, light-weight and absorbent. Good shape retention. Look and feel of wool. Resists mildew, moths, chemicals, and sunlight. May pill.	Machine wash, wrong side out (to avoid pilling) 3 minutes in lukewarm water. Drip dry or dry on flat surface. If needed, press lightly when dry on wrong side with warm iron. Do not remove from ironing board until cool.
Modacrylic	Deep-pile fleece and fur-like coats Lining Robes	Resists wrinkles, moths, mildew, chemicals, and sunlight. Non-allergenic. Quick-drying.	Dry cleaning recommended.
Nylon	Swimwear Dresses Blouses Lingerie Lining Rib trim	Strong, resilient. Dyes well, good color fastness. Will not pill. Low sun resistance.	Machine wash 3 minutes in warm water. Tumble dry on low setting or drip dry. Use cool iron on wrong side of fabric.
Polyester	Dresses Pants Blouses Men's wear Skirts Tops Uniforms Children's wear	Wrinkle resistant. Good recovery if wrinkles do occur. Resists stretching or sagging. Long wearing. Low moisture absorbency.	Machine wash, perma press cycle. Tumble dry at a cool or warm setting for 20-25 minutes. Never use hot iron for pressing.

| Qiana | Loungewear. Lingerie. Scarves. Ties. Dresses. Blouses. Shirts. | Only synthetic that "breathes" like a natural fiber. Hand of silk. Resists water spotting, wrinkling, fading, and shrinking. | Hand or machine wash in warm water. Tumble dry at low temperature, or drip dry. Remove immediately from dryer. Iron on "low wool" setting. Use press cloth and allow fabric to cool on board before removing. Can be dry cleaned. |

Man-Made Fibers

Generic Name	Use	Characteristics	Care
Acetate	Linings Blouses Dresses Backing for bonded fabric	Drapes well. Strong when dry. Dries quickly, holds crease well. Poor abrasion resistance. Heat sensitive.	Dry cleaning recommended. If labeled washable, wash in lukewarm water for 3 minutes. Spin. When evenly damp, use warm iron with press cloth to iron dry. Will dissolve in acetone (fingernail polish remover).
Triacetate	Blouses Knit tops Lingerie Tennis wear	Drapes well. Resists fading, shrinking, wrinkling, and heat. Creases and pleats well.	Machine wash, warm. When evenly damp, use warm iron with press cloth to iron dry. Will dissolve in acetone (fingernail polish remover).
Rayon	Dresses Blouses Lingerie	Lustrous, cool, will not pill. Absorbent. Drapes well. Low wrinkle resistance. Loses body in washing.	Dry cleaning recommended. If labeled machine wash, wash in lukewarm water 3 minutes. Spin out excess water. When evenly damp, use warm iron on wrong side to dry.

Index

A

B

C